Defense Politics

Arnold Kanter

Defense Politics
A budgetary perspective

The University of Chicago Press
Chicago and London

The University of Chicago Press, Chicago 60637
The University of Chicago Press, Ltd., London

Published 1979
Paperback edition 1983
Printed in the United States of America
90 89 88 87 86 85 84 83   2 3 4 5 6

Library of Congress Cataloging in Publication Data

Kanter, Arnold.
  Defense politics.

  Bibliography: p.
  Includes index.
  1. United States—National security.
2. Budget—United States. 3. United States.
Dept. of Defense—Appropriations and expenditures.
4. Civil supremacy over the military—United
States. I. Title.
UA23.K34   353.6   78-21848
ISBN 0-226-42373-5   (cloth)
       0-226-42374-3   (paper)

Contents

Acknowledgments   vii

Introduction   **1**

1. The National Security Policy Process   **3**
A Budgetary Perspective

2. The Organizational Structure of the "Military"   **14**
Identifying Bureaucratic Boundaries

3. Interaction among Participants   **24**
Incentives for Interservice Cooperation and Conflict

4. Interaction among Participants   **45**
Patterns of Military Support for Administration Policies

5. Budget-making as Policy-making   **59**
The Intended Consequences

6. Budget-making as Policy-making   **79**
The Unintended Consequences

7. Military Subordinates as Policy Allies   **95**
Eliciting Compliance

8. Conclusion   **118**

Notes   125

References   141

Index   149

Acknowledgments

One of the infrequently acknowledged benefits of procrastination is the increased opportunity to learn from others before committing oneself. In the present case, I have incurred the burden of a vast opportunity. The extent to which this potential has been exploited remains arguable. By contrast, my debt and gratitude to others are clear.

This study began while I was a research fellow at the Brookings Institution. Brookings not only provided me with financial support and an opportunity to live in Washington but also—if unintentionally—with Morton Halperin, who focused my interests and educated me in the daily realities of bureaucratic decision-making and conflicts. He also arranged for me to remain at Brookings for a second year, masquerading as his research assistant but in reality continuing as his subsidized student. During those two years, he helped me to strengthen the bridge between my academic training and the policy problems which fascinated me. From the beginning, he nurtured my curiosity, endured my impertinence, and indulged my naiveté. Not only did I acquire new knowledge and an enriched perspective, but I gained a valued colleague and close friend.

My graduate training at Yale University provided indispensable preparation. I not only was instructed in the tools and perspective of systematic empirical inquiry but also in the difference between sterile pedantry and good social science. Joseph LaPalombara taught me these lessons in the classroom and insisted on them during the research which formed the basis of this book. He also combined invaluable direction and encouragement with an almost unlimited tolerance for my delays and diversions.

The research was completed and much of the writing was done at the University of Michigan—where my interest in political science and international relations began as an undergraduate—when Pat Crecine made me an offer I couldn't refuse. His enthusiasm and guidance, and the support of the people at the university's Institute of Public Policy Studies, greatly improved the product and facilitated the result. My former professors in the Department of Political Science at Michigan continued their seemingly futile effort to educate me, this time as a colleague.

Acknowledgments

In January 1977, I joined the Bureau of Politico-Military Affairs in the Department of State where I gained firsthand experience in bureaucratic politics and national security policy. Fortunately, all of the research for this book had been completed by that time. As a result, my time in the State Department has contributed little more to this volume than additional delays in getting it into print.

My wife, Anne, contributed a healthy detachment as well as considerable affection. Through it all, she managed never to confuse the roles of companion and colleague. My daughter, Clare, paid a high price in playtime foregone. Since this book has been part of her life from the beginning, however, she may be alone in finding its completion disruptive. Noah, by contrast, had the good sense to wait until it was over.

In keeping with the tradition of such things, I thank all of these people for their help and absolve them of any responsibility for my failure to benefit more. The reader nevertheless may ask why, in view of all of this assistance, the book is not better. That is a good question.

Introduction

In his memoir of the Cuban missile crisis, Robert Kennedy said about his brother (1969, p. 95): "The President believed he was President and that, his wishes having been made clear, they would be followed." As the new president discovered at the height of the missile crisis, however, his previous orders had not been followed and U.S. missiles had not been removed from Turkey.

Kennedy's apparently genuine surprise notwithstanding, scholarly case studies and participants' memoirs routinely give the lie to the assumption that the formal hierarchy describes the organizational reality of the U.S. foreign policy process. Neustadt's classic study (1960) portrays occupants of the "most powerful office in the world" as politicians who are constrained by circumstances and are heavily dependent upon their nominal subordinates in the bureaucracy. He shows (1973) that behind the myth of "presidents-in-boots" lurks the reality of "presidents-in-sneakers" who struggle to get the government that they purport to lead to consent to follow.[1] They must constantly bargain and compromise, as well as command and threaten, in order to narrow the gap between their intentions and the actions which are taken in their name. They virtually never are completely successful.

This widely accepted view also has important implications for the analysis of international relations. Interactions among international actors are not dialogues between two sensible individuals. Rather, they are exchanges among collections of individuals and groups more or less structured by, and responsive to, formal organizational networks. Neustadt's description of relations among allies (1970, pp. ix–x) applies a fortiori to interactions among adversaries:

> relationships between allies . . . are relationships of vast machines with different histories, routines, preoccupations, [and] prospects. . . . If one government would influence the actions of another, it must find means to convince enough men and the right men on the other side that what it wants is what they need for their own purposes, in their own jobs, comporting with their own internally inspired hopes and fears, so that they will pursue it for themselves in their own bargaining arena.

The analysis of "politics among nations," in brief, begins with an appreciation of politics *within* nations.

Thus, the interests of students of international relations converge with the concerns of decision-makers: a scholarly analysis of the determinants of the decisions and actions which represent a nation's behavior in the international arena may be structured in part by the participants' concerns and perspectives. Both scholars and practitioners are concerned with the *problems* which confront politically accountable decision-makers as they seek to translate their policy preferences into behavior, the *means* by which they attempt to overcome these obstacles, and the *successes and failures* which they experience. Accordingly, policy theories (Kanter and Thorson 1972) of international interactions begin with an appreciation of the struggle to shape the decisions and actions which constitute a nation's foreign policy.[2] The present study addresses these issues in the context of the defense policy process in the United States from 1953 to 1969. Specifically, it is concerned with the interaction between presidential administrations and the military services within the framework of the defense budget-making process.

The study's central premise is that the *process* which generates the annual defense budget encompasses and reflects a substantial proportion of the interactions between the military services and the incumbent presidential administration. The *outcomes* of the budget process, indicated by the provisional resource allocations at various stages of each annual budget cycle and across time, offer quantitative evidence of the results of interactions among participants. The formal budgeting *rules*, finally, are viewed as having significant consequences for the probability as well as the form of noncompliance.

This "budgetary perspective" will be the lens through which the efforts of recent presidential administrations to manage the participation of the military services in the defense policy process will be viewed and evaluated. The record of the "McNamara Revolution" in the Pentagon will be compared with the experiences of the Eisenhower administration to illuminate the mechanisms of organizational control attempted by each administration, and to evaluate the results—both intended and unanticipated—that each produced. Specifically, decision-making by the Joint Chiefs of Staff, developments in strategic doctrine, changes in the distribution of resources, and trends in the promotion probabilities of career military officers will be analyzed from a "budgetary perspective." The purpose throughout is to discover by what means, and with what success, incumbent administrations have sought convergence between their policy preferences and the behavior of their subordinates in uniform.

1

The National Security Policy Process
A Budgetary Perspective

The world of decision-makers pursuing multiple goals in an organizational context is, to varying degrees, structured by the process of resource allocation—the rules of the budget cycle.[1] The outcomes of that interaction are reflected in the allocations which emerge—the periodic budgets which direct and constrain the behavior of the departments and agencies. As Frederick Mosher (1954) has observed:

> The grades, ranks, compensation and specializations of personnel; the methods and procedures of working together; the goals and aspirations of groups; the accustomed patterns of formal and informal organization; the configurations of power within the organization; and even the missions and established programs—all of these affect and are affected by the budget.

On the one hand, budgets can *track* the policy process and *record* substantive policy outcomes. Although the decision processes which produce "policy" often are diverse and only loosely coordinated, they all tend to leave traces in the annual budget cycle. Policy choices are associated with alternative distributions of scarce resources. Policy decisions are reflected as the successful budgetary claims made by some agencies and programs at the expense of others. Ideally, therefore, budget data reveal the preferences and priorities of participants. The regular stages of budget formulation and implementation track the interaction among the players and record the outcomes of the struggles that occur (Wildavsky 1968).

For the policy-maker, this means that many of the major issues and controversies will routinely surface at regular intervals for his consideration; an important part of the decision agenda is reliably set as a by-product of the annual budget cycle (Mosher 1954, p. 11). For the analyst, a budgetary perspective is a potentially fruitful approach to understanding the organizational context of policy-making and to assessing politically accountable decision-makers' success in achieving their objectives (Schilling 1962, p. 15).

On the other hand, budgeting can actively *shape* substantive policy outcomes. The budgetary process yields unequal distributions of rewards and bargaining advantages as well as resources. Not only do direct and personal rewards such as salaries consume resources,

3

but the symbols of many intangible rewards such as prestige and esteem are themselves tangible—and expensive (Downs 1967, p. 196). Moreover, bureaucrats' personal and programmatic incentives frequently are responsive to changes in their organizational environment which bear on the patterns and conditions of resource availability. A politically accountable decision-maker, therefore, would be well advised to consider an organizational strategy to achieve preferred decisions and actions that was based upon, and operated through, domination of the formal budget system (Lindblom 1955, p. 24).

A Budgetary Perspective on the Department of Defense

The annual budget is the time for decision (Schultze 1968, p. 24). As one Navy officer explained, there is a pervasive tendency in the Pentagon to postpone decisions, to keep the options open, and to avoid conflict.[2] The annual budget cycle, since it *forces* decisions, is a major locus of influence: "No one gets serious about deciding anything until the budget is due." One Air Force officer observed: "The budget-makers, who allocate the budget and the budget reductions, are, in one sense, running the Air Force."

The extent to which the defense policy process is encompassed by the budget cycle appears to be well understood by the participants themselves. The military services pay very close attention to their budgets, in absolute size and in relation to those of their sister services (Halperin 1971, pp. 86–87). All of the officers interviewed knew the size and allocations of their service's budget for that year, although, for many, their formal responsibilities neither required nor encouraged familiarity with such data. They also knew their service's *share* of the total defense budget, the shares of the other services, and the respective budget shares in the recent past. The importance attached to budgetary issues by the participants is underscored by the fact that several of these officers also acknowledged that the budgeting system introduced under McNamara (and continued with important modifications by his successors) should have made service budget shares an inappropriate guide for behavior and an inaccurate measure of organizational success.

The civilians devote corresponding attention to the same criteria. Former Deputy Secretary of Defense David Packard, who supervised the budget cycle during his tenure in the Nixon administration, required that each service's *share* of the budget being prepared be included in the information sent up for his review.

Defense budgets reflect two related, but distinct, concerns. First, the magnitude of budgetary support is perceived to be intrinsically important. President Nixon and Henry Kissinger believed that the aggregate level of defense expenditures is an important signal to foreign nations of U.S. resolve. They are reported to have insisted, for this reason, that the defense budget in some years be increased, although they were somewhat less interested in which defense programs were the beneficiaries of the additional resources (confidential interview). For the military services, the size of their budgets —both absolutely and relative to those of the other services—is a measure of organizational success (Grosse and Proschan 1967, p. 26).

Second, defense budgets reflect the military capabilities that define the Pentagon's national security mission, the organizational objectives of the services, and the outcomes of the interactions among participants with different program priorities. Robert McNamara probably stated this position most forcefully: "policy decisions must sooner or later be expressed in the form of budget decisions on where to spend and how much" (quoted in Enthoven and Smith 1971, p. 35). A comparison of the budget estimates that the services submit to the secretary with the defense budget that the president presents to Congress reveals to the services which among them succeeded and which failed. From the president's perspective, the comparison indicates how successful politically accountable civilians have been in imposing their view of the requirements of national security on the uniformed bureaucracy.

The budget cycle not only drives much of the policy process, but the formal budgeting system which defines that cycle also distributes bargaining resources unequally among the participants and produces differences in ability to influence outcomes. Mosher, for example, has noted (1954, p. 88) how the Army's move to a "performance budget" in the late 1940s was accompanied by a reduction in the autonomy and influence of the Army technical services and a concomitant growth in the decision-making power of the General Staff. He concludes that, regardless of the intent behind the decision to alter the budgeting system, "In fact, this [redistribution of power] would appear to be the most important effect of the new system." Similarly, Stephen Riordan (1958) has described the Navy's (largely successful) resistance during the 1950s to changes in the budget structure which it viewed as threats to the autonomy of its bureaus.

From the perspective of the services, the rules for budget preparation represent the complex system of obstacles and incentives which intervene between their objectives and fulfillment. From the perspective of the administration, the procedures which regulate the preparation of the annual defense budget are a fundamental mechanism by which to impose its view of national security on the direction of spending. Precisely because the direction of the national defense is substantially determined by the pattern of spending, and because substantive policy outcomes are sensitive to the budget process, civilian control over the allocation of resources is the long lever by which politically accountable officials have sought to implement their understanding of the requirements of national security.

The importance of the budgeting process for the control of defense policy was recognized as early as the 1949 amendments to the National Security Act. According to Walter Millis, "the core of the whole problem, as Forrestal clearly saw after the almost grotesque experiences of the spring [of 1948], lay in the budget" (quoted in Mosher 1954, p. 32n). The amendments to the original 1947 legislation attempted to enhance the secretary's power by vesting in him full authority over the preparation of the defense budget. Not only was the Department of Defense established, but the position of comptroller was created.[3] Ferdinand Eberstadt testified in support of these amendments: "The budget is one of the most effective, if not the strongest, implements of civilian control over the military establishment" (quoted in Lucas and Dawson 1974, p. 127).

A decade later, the architects of the McNamara Revolution continued to share with the Hoover Commission (which proposed the 1949 amendments) the belief that budget outcomes are the quantitative statement of defense policy. This view of the budgetary process as a vehicle for policy control formed the core of McNamara's criticism of his predecessors and the basis of his plans for reform (McNamara 1968; Hitch 1965). The budget procedures of the 1950s were portrayed as crude in design, blunt in effect, and, most important, incapable of being exploited by the political leadership to exercise control over the direction of national security policy. The annual budget cycle was to be the battlefield of the McNamara Revolution. Its hallmark was to be the Planning-Programming-Budgeting System (PPBS) which regulated the preparation of the defense budget.

Description of the Budget Data
Defense budget data from the Eisenhower, Kennedy, and Johnson administrations will form the basis of my analysis. Data from three of the major stages in the annual budget cycle are included:[4] (a) the

services' budget estimates submitted to the secretary of defense early in the October preceding the beginning of the fiscal year for which the budget has been prepared; (b) the president's budget requests presented to Congress in January; and (c) the appropriations agreed to in the House-Senate conference committee and enacted into law.[5] All data are in terms of New Obligational Authority and are reported in current dollars (that is, not adjusted for inflation).

Although "program" budgets would be more useful, the necessary data only are available in a "line-item" format.[6] Even in the latter format, disaggregation of the total service budgets helps to identify changes in resource allocations among budget stages and across time. Moreover, several of the line items are associated with a relatively high level of functional specificity, e.g., "Aircraft Procurement, Air Force," and "Shipbuilding and Conversion, Navy." These data permit certain inferences such as the priority which various participants attach to ships and planes and to the military missions performed by each.[7] The line-items included in the FY 1969 budget are listed in table 1.

Much of the analysis will focus on differences in the budget requests among the budget stages, and changes in the distribution of funds among categories between stages. To avoid the problem of comparing service requests prepared under one administration with the presidential budget requests submitted to Congress by its successor, transition years ordinarily are excluded: the Eisenhower administration will be defined as the period from FY 1955 to FY 1961 and the Kennedy-Johnson administration (and, for convenience, McNamara's tenure as secretary of defense) will be defined as FY 1963 to FY 1969. For those cases in which transition years are included, the presidential budget requests are those of the *incoming* administration—Eisenhower for FY 1954 and Kennedy for FY 1962. For the purposes of the budgetary analysis, the Vietnam war begins in FY 1967 when the incremental costs of the conflict first were acknowledged.

Included in presidential budget requests are those *amendments* which the administration added after the budget was formally presented to Congress but before appropriations were voted. These amendments are significant only in the presidential transitions years. *Supplementals* to the budget are not included in the analysis for two reasons. First, except during wartime, the supplementals involved small amounts of money (relative to the basic defense budget) designated for noncontroversial purposes such as family housing and mandated pay increases.[8] Second, and for present purposes

Table 1. Line Items in FY 1969 Defense Budget

Military Personnel

Military Personnel, Army
Military Personnel, Navy
Military Personnel, Marine Corps
Military Personnel, Air Force
Reserve Personnel, Army
Reserve Personnel, Navy
Reserve Personnel, Marine Corps
Reserve Personnel, Air Force
National Guard Personnel, Army
National Guard Personnel, Air Force
Retired Pay, Defense

Operation and Maintenance

Operation and Maintenance, Army
Operation and Maintenance, Navy
Operation and Maintenance, Marine Corps
Operation and Maintenance, Air Force
Operation and Maintenance, Defense Agencies
Operation and Maintenance, Army National Guard
Operation and Maintenance, Air National Guard
National Board for the Promotion of Rifle Practice, Army[a]
Claims, Defense
Contingencies, Defense
Court of Military Appeals, Defense

Procurement

Procurement of Equipment and Missiles, Army
Procurement of Aircraft and Missiles, Navy
Shipbuilding and Conversion, Navy
Other Procurement, Navy
Procurement, Marine Corps
Aircraft Procurement, Air Force
Missile Procurement, Air Force
Other Procurement, Air Force
Procurement, Defense Agencies

Research, Development, Test, and Evaluation

Research, Development, Test, and Evaluation, Army
Research, Development, Test, and Evaluation, Navy
Research, Development, Test, and Evaluation, Air Force

Table 1—*Continued*

Research, Development, Test, and Evaluation, Defense Agencies
Emergency Fund, Defense

Military Construction

Military Construction, Army
Military Construction, Navy
Military Construction, Air Force
Military Construction, Defense Agencies
Military Construction, Army Reserve
Military Construction, Navy Reserve
Military Construction, Air Force Reserve
Military Construction, Army National Guard
Military Construction, Air National Guard
Loran Stations, Defense[a]

Family Housing[a]

Civil Defense[a]

[a]Not included in analysis.

more important, supplementals are generated and processed by mechanisms separate from the budgeting systems we will be considering.[9]

Since the disaggregated budget at each stage is a record of the priorities and objectives of the participants involved as well as a reflection of the interactions among them, the data indicate some combination of a priori preferences and the results of clashes and compromises. For example, the final service budget estimates to the secretary reveal only the outcome of the intraservice process: indications of the range of intraservice objectives are confounded with the intraservice distribution of bargaining advantages. Similarly, the president's budget requests to the Congress combine the national security preferences of the administration with the results of its interactions with the military services.

Organization of the Study
Following the description of the organizational structure of the "military" in Chapter 2, these budget data are used to interpret and evaluate the organizational politics of national security policy since 1953. Chapters 3 and 4 use budget data to track and explain the behavior of military and civilian participants. Based on the record

of unanimous and split recommendations made by the Joint Chiefs of Staff, Chapter 3 discusses the incentives for cooperation and competition among the military services. Chapter 4 addresses the same topics with regard to civil-military interactions.

Chapters 5 through 7 examine efforts to use the budget process to shape defense policy. Chapter 5 assesses the formal budget-making process as an instrument of policy control during the Eisenhower and Kennedy-Johnson administrations in terms of the criteria invoked by the advocates of PPBS—introduced in the Department of Defense in the early 1960s. Chapter 6 examines some of the unanticipated consequences of PPBS and its predecessors. Chapter 7 assays the opportunities to elicit compliance indirectly by exploiting the military services' responsiveness to budget-induced changes in their organizational environments.

Appendix: Utility of the Budgetary Perspective

The fruitfulness of a "budgetary perspective," both as a research strategy and policy instrument, will vary from organization to organization. The payoffs will depend upon (a) the extent to which budget allocations reflect participants' preferences and goals, (b) the extent to which behavior is responsive to variations in the level and distribution of resources, per se, and (c) the concentration or diffusion of decision-making authority regarding resource allocation.

The ability of analysts and decision-makers to associate budget allocations with program choices depends in part on the budget *format*, that is, the categories in terms of which appropriations and expenditures are distributed and aggregated. The benefits and disadvantages of alternative budget formats have been addressed in the context of criticisms of "input budgeting" and advocacy of "program budgeting."

Input budgeting refers to budget categories that are related to the resources, or "inputs," available to the organization to undertake its activities (Merewitz and Sosnick 1971, p. 22). The format in which the defense budget is presented to Congress is an example of input budgeting. The names of the appropriations titles are suggestive: Military Personnel; Operation and Maintenance; Procurement; Research, Development, Test, and Evaluation; and Military Construction. The problem with such a format is that it may be difficult to associate budget outlays with the organization's purposes. Likewise, the association between changes in the level of appropriations devoted to these objects of expenditures and changes in the policies and preferences of the participants may be problematical.

To ameliorate these shortcomings, an alternative budget format has been proposed—and to some extent implemented—which aggregates resource allocations in categories that "are closer to being true outputs than the older categories" (McKean and Anshen 1967, p. 338). These organizational outputs are the organization's programs defined as "combinations of activities that produce distinguishable products" (Hitch and McKean 1966, p. 49). The program budget introduced by Secretary of Defense McNamara in the early 1960s for the preparation of the defense budget within the executive branch is an example of output budgeting. The avowed purpose of this format is to encourage an explicit consideration of alternative organizational objectives and alternative means to the same end (Enthoven and Smith 1971, pp. 38–42). To the extent that an organization's budget data are aggregated into categories which approximate its "true outputs," resource allocation decisions can be related to choices among alternative organizational activities and objectives. Correspondingly, the organization's choice between budget formats will influence the analyst's ability to associate budget analyses with organizational behavior and the outcomes of interactions.

However, the strength of association between resource allocations and choices among alternative organizational activities to some extent is independent of the formal budget format (cf. Schick 1967, p. 48). In particular, to the extent that budget categories coincide with the interests and goals of different participants in the decision-making process, the analyst can make inferences regarding program priorities and the outcome of interaction among participants—regardless of the budget format. For example, if each of several components of an organization has a relatively distinct and distinctive mission, budgeting in terms of these components provides good insights into the relationship between budgets and objectives. Thus, William Niskanen argues (1967, p. 6) that, at least through the years of World War II, each of the military services had a primary mission which was different from, and performed in substantial independence of, the missions of the other services. Under these circumstances, aggregating outlays in terms of organizational subunit (that is, each military service)—which was the format in use through the 1950s—is a useful way to relate resource allocations to decisions regarding alternative defense strategies.

Since it is difficult to gauge the organization's choices among alternatives from resources allocated to salaries and wages, analyzing personnel budgets may be a relatively unpromising way to map the organization's goals. For example, a large proportion of the State Department budget is consumed by the salaries paid to its employees and the expenses entailed by operating embassies and consulates throughout the world. The clashes among the participants within State rarely occur over the allocation of its appropriation, and the struggles over policy are only infrequently reflected in its budget requests (Schelling 1970, p. 112). An analysis of the State Department's budget and budgetary process should, therefore, have only modest payoffs.

By contrast, some "objects of expenditure" are characterized by relatively high functional specificity. For example, the format in which the defense budget currently is presented to Congress identifies the direct acquisition costs of missiles, aircraft, and ships. Although these expenditures still are not readily relatable to specific defense programs, it is possible to make inferences regarding choices among alternative defense postures from changes in allocations among these categories. More generally, we would expect the budgetary perspective to have lower payoffs in an analysis of organizations whose budgets primarily are consumed by (functionally diffuse) wages, salaries, and administrative overhead than in analysis of organizations whose tasks require large (functionally specific) expenditures in addition to those required for manpower.

The budgetary implications of alternative courses of action also are likely to be more salient in the latter type of organization: the allocation and distribution of resources acquire *intrinsic* importance. The smaller the proportion of the organization's budget accounted for by payroll, the stronger the relationship between the level of resources available and the organization's presumptive ability to achieve its objectives (however and by whomever defined). Accordingly, there will be an increased probability that issues will be evaluated by all of the participants in terms of the consequences for changes in the level and distribution of resources, whether or not such choices formally are "budgetary" decisions.

As a corollary, decisions which formally bear on resources will be perceived by the participants to be increasingly consequential (Halperin 1971, pp. 75–76). We would expect the budgetary process to reflect a greater proportion of the total interactions in such organizations and we would expect its subordinates to be more responsive to budgetary threats and promises.

Finally, the analytical payoffs associated with a budgetary perspective are directly related to the amount of allocational discretion which resides within the organization. For example, a department's discretion is limited to the extent that its budget is devoted to fiscally "uncontrollable" expenditures—outlays legally required by previous legislation or formulas over which the department has no direct short-term control. Thus, a very large proportion of the annual budget for the Department of Health, Education, and Welfare (HEW) is accounted for by Social Security trust funds and matching grants to states. Such expenditures are beyond the control of the department, the president, or indeed the Congress in the absence of changes in legislation. Murray Weidenbaum (1970, p. 240) has estimated that only about 12 percent of the HEW budget in FY 1969 was "relatively controllable." By contrast, 97 percent of the military component of the Defense Department budget in that year was classified as relatively controllable. (One should be careful to distinguish the proportion of a department's budget which is *legally* uncontrollable from the often much larger percentage which—as in the Defense Department—is substantially immune to change in the short run [Marshall 1966, pp. 14–15]).

Alternatively, authority over allocations might simply reside elsewhere in the political system. One indication of a federal department's allocational discretion is given by the level of detail included in congressional appropriations acts. As Charles Schultze notes (1968, p. 4), the annual funding for the Defense Department is about five times as large as HEW's budget (exclusive of trust funds), but the Pentagon's budget is approved by Congress in about half the number of appropriations. By implication, HEW has less discretion over allocation of its resources than does the Pentagon.

Although it may be possible to associate resource allocations with organizational activities in bureaucracies such as HEW, inferences from those patterns of spending to the organizational participants' priorities and successes are less direct and more tenuous (cf. Greenberg 1972). Accordingly, analyses of budget processes and outcomes in such organizations may range from unrewarding to misleading. The characteristics of the Pentagon, by contrast, indicate that an investigation of defense budgets and budgeting will yield considerable insights into the national security policy process. As Mosher observed in 1954 (p. vii): "My explorations within the Department of Defense have impressed me, perhaps more than anything else, with the interrelatedness of budgeting with virtually everything else that affects policy and administration."

2

The Organizational Structure of the "Military"
Identifying Bureaucratic Boundaries

March and Simon (1958, p. 1) wisely counsel that the troublesome problem of defining the term "organization" be avoided. We confront a related problem, however, for which no such easy escape seems possible. The study of efforts by postwar administrations to direct the behavior of their uniformed subordinates, and of interactions among those military participants, requires some guidelines for establishing where one military organization ends and another begins. Does the president have to negotiate with the "military" en masse, can he seek an alliance with one service as he bargains with another, or can he appeal to one intraservice group at the expense of another? An analysis of the organizational politics of national security policy, in brief, virtually demands some heuristics for determining organizational *boundaries.*[1]

We are concerned with organizational boundaries in part because they give structure to the patterns of interactions among participants, making some interactions more likely than others. We are also concerned with identifying dominant boundaries for the light they shed on identifying communities of interest and on the probabilities of organizationally generated conflict among participants. To the extent that a boundary is dominant (relative to alternative boundaries), we would expect a greater probability of compromise and cooperation within it, and a lower probability of compromise and cooperation with groups beyond it. The structure of competition within the military, for example, will affect *which* national security issues and information come to the president's attention. Accordingly, he is concerned with predicting—and influencing—which differences among his uniformed subordinates are likely to be submerged and which are likely to generate conflict.

Organizational cleavages are neither unique nor permanent. They tend to be variable in that different problems—both research and policy—affect the significance of alternative boundaries (Cyert and March 1963, p. 27; Downs 1967, p. 211). More important, the budgetary analysis presented below demonstrates that these cleavages are manipulable in that participants' sense of community and the dimensions of competition among them can be changed. Notwithstanding this relativity of organizational distinctions, however, the *formal* bureaucratic structure provides the starting point for behaviorally drawn organizational boundaries. It contributes to and reflects identifications which influence the probabilities and the patterns of competition and collusion.

Organizational Boundaries: The "Military" as an Organization

It perhaps should be emphasized that the "military" is, at best, an analytical distinction without a definitive organizational embodiment. When the president's policies and decisions depend upon the planned or actual use of physical violence, there is no single organizational entity called the "military" to which he can turn. The chairman of the Joint Chiefs of Staff (JCS) does not formally represent the "military" since he has no legal authority over the other members. The JCS itself is not the corporate representative of the "military" so much as it is a committee of representatives from the individual services; when the individual members of the JCS (except the chairman) "change their hats," they are the chiefs of the three military services.

Even when they carry out their primary JCS responsibility of giving advice to the president, the Chiefs predominantly depend upon their individual service staffs. In preparation for JCS meetings, the members (except the chairman) are briefed by their respective service staffs rather than by the Joint Staff on issues and positions. When the Joint Chiefs cannot reach unanimous agreement, dissents customarily are prepared by the service staffs:

> the last thing a chief does before walking into a JCS meeting is to receive a thorough briefing by a senior member of his service staff, the operations deputy, who has earlier been briefed, with strongly supported recommendations, by working-level staff officers from his particular service. This custom has changed little, if at all, in over twenty years. [Legere and Davis 1969b, pp. 212–13]

Officers can and have overcome the distinctions among the services to behave as the "military." The Joint Chiefs of Staff, however, are less an organizational embodiment of the military than an *arena* in which the services interact. While the JCS is an important formal mechanism which facilitates that interaction, the few procedures and structures which promote a sense of a common identity tend to be overwhelmed by the traditions and structures which emphasize their differences. There are few devices for enforcing agreement save mutual self-interest. A president who depends upon his military subordinates may be compelled—or have the opportunity —to negotiate with the individual services.

Organizational Boundaries: Military Services as Independent Organizations

The Army, the Navy, and even the Air Force, antedate the Department of Defense as formal organizations. Accordingly, the latecomer Defense Department was superimposed upon separate, ongoing organizations and existing patterns of interaction. Moreover, there is a striking absence of mechanisms at the Department of Defense level which would disrupt and replace these patterns. Indeed, there is virtually no activity or function which includes all Department of Defense personnel. Far from having a common chain of command and promotion structure, the Department of Defense does not even have shared security clearances or a single housekeeping service.

On the contrary, all three military services are called "departments" and successive reorganizations of the Pentagon have given special attention to preserving the essential distinctions symbolized by the nomenclature. The 1949 amendments to the National Security Act, while reducing the services from "executive departments" to "military departments," prohibited the secretary of defense from achieving substantial unification by requiring that they be "separately administered." The 1958 amendments, likewise motivated by a concern about interservice rivalries, nevertheless required that the services continue to be "separately organized."[2] Information processing, budget formulation, and role socialization continue to be organized in terms of the separate services.

Perhaps the most obvious, but still significant, symbol of differences which the participants themselves consider to be important is the military uniform. Not only do the uniforms differentiate military from civilians, but they also distinguish sharply among the services. By contrast, uniforms and insignia distinguish intraservice groups less frequently and more subtly. The attributes of the military uniform appear to be neither accidental nor trivial: witness the (largely unsuccessful) attempts by McNamara to introduce a modest measure of commonality in the apparel of military officers (cf. Rosser 1973; Kaufman 1960, pp. 183–85).

If the uniform is the symbol, the structure of positive and negative sanctions is the substance which distinguishes one service from another. Members of a military service are subject to the same chain of command and to the same promotion structure, neither of which is shared with the other services. The participants' incentives, especially as these are influenced by the allocation of rewards and punishments, lead to an identification with their individual service and strengthen the bonds of identity with, and loyalty to, it (Downs 1967, pp. 211–12).[3]

The salience of the service as the predominant source of sanctions and focus of identification is highlighted by the history of formal reorganizations which cut across service boundaries. For example, the 1958 amendments to the National Security Act formalized the concept of multiservice "unified" and "specified" commands and removed the military departments from the chain of command over operating forces. However, the U.S. Blue Ribbon Defense Panel reported in 1970 (pp. 47–48) that the de facto organization of the combat functions continued to conform to the structure of the incentive system, that is, the individual military services, rather than to the official organization of the combatant commands which cut across service lines:

> very few Navy forces are assigned to Unified Commands in which the Unified Commander is not a Naval Officer, except for the 6th Fleet assigned to EUCOM. Equally significant, all of the Army forces in PACOM, which are commanded by a Naval Officer, fall under sub-unified commands commanded by other than Naval officers and the overwhelming proportion of Army forces in PACOM fall under sub-unified commands which are commanded by Army officers.

Similarly, the Navy's missile-firing submarines are not assigned to the Strategic Air Command, the combatant command with responsibility for strategic warfare missions (but which always has been commanded by an Air Force general).

Indeed, the Panel (1970, p. 50) concluded that, notwithstanding the successive reorganizations of the Defense Department, the relationships between commanders of operational forces and the military services "remain substantially unchanged." Its findings confirm the importance of the military services as the predominant source of sanctions and focus of organizational loyalty. The experience of the combatant commands illustrates the limited impact of formal organizational changes superimposed on (and insensitive to) the existing patterns of interaction and constellation of incentives which the participants confront. The military services monopolize the allocation of present and future sanctions. Alternative formal organizations, for example, combatant commands and defense agencies, let alone purely analytical distinctions such as the "military," are weak competitors for the officers' loyalties and, consequently, are weak candidates for alternative organizational boundaries.

Organizational Boundaries: Intraservice Distinctions

Interservice cleavages ordinarily will dominate intraservice distinctions: the service-wide system of authority and sanctions, combined with the military tradition of obedience to orders and emphasis on strict hierarchy, should do much of the president's work for him below these levels (Huntington 1961b, p. 51). Each of the services, however, is itself a complex organization composed of numerous subsidiary units and components. For example, the Strategic Air Command (especially its bomber pilots), fighter and attack pilots, and transport pilots were identified during interviews as some of the major Air Force factions. Naval aviators, submariners, and the "ship drivers" of the surface fleets are prominent groups within the Navy (Halperin 1971; Huntington 1961a, pp. 405–6).

Just as uniforms differentiate among the services, particular insignia distinguish among members within a service. Thus, aviators in the Air Force wear wings on their uniforms, aviators in the Navy were entitled to wear brown shoes (rather than black) until the early 1970s, and each branch of the Army is identified by characteristic insignia. Moreover, these differences are important to the members of each service. In particular, promotions to higher rank typically are reported (albeit unofficially) in terms of a variety of intraservice distinctions.

A picture of the tension between intraservice and service loyalties is presented by examining the locus of organizational loyalties of aviators in the various services: do they consider themselves to be primarily *pilots* or rather to be members of the *military service* to which they belong?

The struggle of the Army Air Forces to secure organizational autonomy from the Army during World War II, superbly documented by Perry Smith (1970), gives a clear answer in one case. In that study, Smith generalizes (p. 23):

> In a large military service, the primary identification is usually with an arm of that service and not with the service itself (a man is a submariner, a naval aviator, a cavalryman, an infantryman) because of the tendency to identify with some smaller and more personal group.

However, Vincent Davis's analysis of the postwar Navy (which traces the rise of the aviators to dominance within the service) reaches an opposite conclusion (1966, p. 120): "the Navy fliers had always been Navy officers first and aviators second." Davis's conclusion raises the possibility that the salience of intraservice distinctions varies among the services.[4]

This was the consensus among those military and civilian officials who were interviewed. There was substantial agreement (including among Army officers) that it was much more difficult to identify salient and stable cleavages which differentiated among well-defined Army groups. Although the informal internal structures of the Navy and Air Force were quickly (and consensually) articulated, some of those interviewed argued that the intra-Navy distinctions were less salient and more easily overcome than those within the Air Force. In essence, these officers and civilians implied that Smith probably was correct with regard to the Air Force while Davis's description of the naval aviators accurately described that situation.

Various explanations for these differences were offered. Some of those interviewed suggested that the salience of intraservice boundaries varies inversely with the opportunities for interaction and/or transfer among intraservice groups during operations (or training for operations).[5] The Army is probably the most closely integrated of the services. There is considerable career mobility among the branches which is facilitated by attendance at the schools of other branches and an organizational structure which has several branches staffing the same Army post. Moreover, combat operations have led to increasing interdependence among the branches, for example, forward observers for artillery accompanying infantry units. Some of those interviewed suggested that, compared to the other services, there is less uniqueness and greater transferability of combat skills among branches in the Army. This may account for the practice of members of one branch commanding units drawn from other branches (cf. Lang 1967, p. 75).[6]

Although combat skills are more distinguishable and less transferable within the Navy, the relatively organic structure of the naval task force leads to considerable interaction and interdependence among the warfare specialties (with the notable exception of missile-firing submarines).[7] By contrast, Air Force combat units often operate in considerable isolation from one another: air wings typically are composed of single "kinds" of aircraft (fighters, transports, etc.) and have distinguishable missions (troop transport, air defense, etc.).[8]

Variation in early professional socialization has been offered as an additional explanation for differences among the military services in the importance of intraservice boundaries. Specifically, under-graduate education at the service academy is thought to predispose an officer to a service-wide perspective and identification (Segal 1967; Segal and Willick 1968). The group loyalty initiated with the academy experience is a sufficiently accepted piece of conventional wisdom to warrant its own descriptive term in the informal vocabulary: academy graduates, especially members of the same graduating class, are commonly (if not always affectionately) referred to as "ring-knockers."

Data on the source of commission for flag-grade officers are consistent with the differences among the services described by the officials interviewed. Segal (1967) provides comparative data for two points in time: 1951 and 1964. As can be seen in table 2, Navy admirals are overwhelmingly, indeed nearly exclusively, Annapolis graduates.[9] In 1951, the composition of the Air Force closely resembled that of the Army, from which it had recently secured its organizational autonomy. By 1964, however, the percentage of Army generals who were academy graduates had increased in every flag rank. In that year, every general and lieutenant general in the Army but two had graduated from West Point.[10] By contrast, the proportion of academy (West Point) graduates among Air Force generals had *declined* in every flag grade except lieutenant general.

The heterogeneity of the early socialization process of Air Force generals is further detailed in table 3. The two data points selected by Segal are part of a long-term trend of a decreasing proportion of Air Force generals with West Point commissions. Thus, in striking contrast to the Navy, and, to a lesser extent, the Army, senior Air Force officers have not been the products of a homogenizing early professional socialization process which might contribute to a service-wide perspective and mitigate the consequences of operations and activities that reinforce intraservice differentiations (Kanter 1977).[11] In sum, the structure of training and operations, in combination with early socialization experiences, leads to the prediction that, ceteris paribus, the Air Force will exhibit the highest level of intraservice differentiation and the Army will demonstrate the least of the three services.

Specifying Civilian Participants

A problem which resembles that of differentiating among military personnel is the identification of the relevant civilian participants. Discussions of the national security policy process in general, and analyses of the tenure of Robert McNamara in particular, ordinar-

Table 2. General Officers of the U.S. Armed Forces by Type of Military Education, 1951 and 1964

Officer Ranks	1951				1964			
	% Academy Graduates	% Nonacademy Graduates	Total %	Total N	% Academy Graduates	% Nonacademy Graduates	Total %	Total N
Army								
General of the Army	75	25[a]	100	4	100	—	100	3
General	75	25[a]	100	4	100	—	100	11
Lieutenant General	61	39	100	18	95	5	100	40
Major General	38[b]	62[a]	100	145	78	22[a]	100	199[c]
Brigadier General	59[b]	42[a]	100	199	68	32	100	249[c]
All general grades	51	49	100	370	75	25	100	502
Navy								
Fleet Admiral	100	—	100	3	100	—	100	1
Admiral	100	—	100	5	100	—	100	7
Vice Admiral	100	—	100	21	100	—	100	31
Rear Admiral	80	20	100	220	87	13	100	252
All admiral grades	82	18	100	249	89	11	100	291
Air Force								
General	75	25	100	4	69	31	100	13
Lieutenant General	31	69	100	13	67	33	100	33
Major General	55	45	100	95	49	51	100	162[c]
Brigadier General	51	49	100	135	23	77	100	214[c]
All General Grades	51	49	100	247	38	62	100	422

Source: David R. Segal, "Selective Promotion in Officer Cohorts," *Sociological Quarterly* 8 (Spring 1967).
[a]Includes "honor schools," such as VMI and Citadel.
[b]Includes one graduate of Annapolis. [c]Based on 50 percent sample.

Table 3: Source of Commission of Air Force General Officers

Year	USMA	ROTC	OCS	Flying Training School	Other	Don't Know	Total	(N)
1953	55.8%	2.4%	0.0%	27.6%	12.7%	1.5%	100%	(333)
1954	54.5	2.5	0.0	28.4	13.0	1.6	100	(363)
1955	53.2	2.8	0.3	29.8	12.1	1.8	100	(389)
1956	53.1	3.8	0.3	29.3	10.9	2.6	100	(392)
1957	51.9	4.7	0.0	29.7	11.4	2.3	100	(387)
1958	52.9	5.4	0.0	27.7	11.4	2.6	100	(390)
1959	51.7	6.3	0.0	28.3	11.6	2.1	100	(382)
1960	49.5	7.1	0.0	28.9	12.9	1.6	100	(380)
1961	43.7	10.5	0.0	31.2	12.6	2.0	100	(391)
1962	41.8	12.1	0.5	32.6	11.5	1.5	100	(390)
1963	36.5	12.9	1.0	38.3	10.0	1.3	100	(394)
1964	35.2	14.4	1.0	40.8	8.4	0.2	100	(395)
1965	31.1	15.3	1.3	45.4	6.9	0.0	100	(392)
1966	28.1	12.7	1.9	52.3	5.1	0.0	100	(377)
1967	27.4	11.0	2.7	54.3	4.6	0.0	100	(372)
1968	24.8	9.2	3.7	57.3	4.8	0.0	100	(379)
1969	24.7	7.1	4.2	58.8	5.3	0.0	100	(381)
1970	27.9	5.9	4.7	56.6	5.0	0.0	100	(387)
1971	27.9	5.1	4.3	58.1	4.6	0.0	100	(391)
1972	27.9	4.9	4.9	57.1	5.4	0.0	100	(350)

Source: *Air Force Register.*

ily concentrate on the position of secretary of defense as the symbol of civilian participation and leadership (for example, Longley 1969; Roherty 1970). This focus has been abetted by the alternative role definitions available to a secretary of defense which McNamara was fond of distinguishing (quoted in Hitch 1965, p. 27):

> He can either act as a judge or a leader. . . . In one case, it's a passive role; in the other case, an active role. . . . I have always believed in and endeavored to follow the active leadership role as opposed to the passive judicial role.

McNamara was, by his criteria, a more active secretary than his predecessors. By contrast, Charles Wilson, Eisenhower's first secretary of defense, was, by all accounts, a "passive" secretary who did not play as dominant a role as did McNamara (Roherty 1970, p. 49; Snyder 1962, pp. 517–18).

The issues of relative "activism" and "strength" exhibited by different administrations will be addressed below. The point here is that a weak secretary does not, ipso facto, entail weak civilian participation. There are other civilians who might substitute for the secretary, most notably, the president himself. That is, Wilson's role definition may have been substantially constrained by the extent of Eisenhower's own participation in defense matters. As Legere and Davis have observed (1969a, p. 175): "President Eisenhower was almost unavoidably his own secretary of defense." Just as the administrations of presidents who considered themselves expert in foreign affairs have been characterized by "weak" secretaries of state, it seems reasonable to expect that a secretary of defense will be more limited in an administration whose president has a special interest in defense matters.

The argument here is *not* that it makes no difference whether the president or his secretary of defense is the primary agent of civilian leadership. The difference seems unavoidable and important (cf. Destler 1972). The claim is more modest: weak and passive secretaries of defense may hold office in active and strong administrations. Accordingly, our attention will not be confined to a comparison among secretaries but rather will seek to compare the role and performance of substantially undifferentiated "civilian administrations."

3

Interaction among Participants
Incentives for Interservice Cooperation and Conflict

The literature includes a welter of loosely related propositions regarding the level of resources, the dimensions of conflict within the national security bureaucracy, and the instruments of civilian control over military policies and practices. Notwithstanding the status of these propositions as parts of the conventional wisdom however, the supporting empirical evidence is modest and frequently contradictory.

The intensity of civil-military conflict usually is thought to be inversely related to the intensity of interservice rivalries (Huntington 1961b, pp. 41–42). Likewise, the position and influence of the civilian political leadership is said to be enhanced in direct relation to the intensity of interservice rivalry: the inability of the services to reach agreement among themselves on policy recommendations both multiplies the administration's policy options and diminishes the military's prestige and political influence (Ginsburgh 1964; Ries 1964, p. 113). Finally, the intensity of interservice rivalry frequently is reputed to be inversely related to the size of the defense budget (Huntington 1961a, pp. 416–17; Taylor 1960, p. 105). Taken together, these relationships suggest that budget policy in its crudest form—controlling the level of resources—is an important instrument of policy control.

It should be noted that these propositions have been derived almost exclusively from an examination of the record prior to 1961. Some students of McNamara's tenure as secretary of defense are led to an implicitly different conclusion regarding the consequences of defense spending. They argue that the increases in the defense budget which occurred during the Kennedy and Johnson administrations muted the services' resistance to McNamara's active involvement in defense policy and inhibited civil-military conflict (Hammond 1968, p. 64; Wildavsky 1970, p. 465).

Accordingly, policy recommendations derived from an analysis of the Eisenhower administration would counsel *reductions* in the defense budget in order to increase civilian influence, while a reading of McNamara's stewardship would suggest budget *increases* to accomplish the same objective. These competing prescriptions can be evaluated by an examination of the relationship between annual changes in the size of the defense budget and variations in the incidence of formal disagreements among the military services.

The Record of Joint Chiefs of Staff Recommendations
As was suggested in Chapter 2, the JCS is the primary arena for interservice negotiations. Studies of the defense policy process often have used the record of official JCS recommendations as an indicator of the character of relations among the services (Huntington 1961a, Taylor 1960). These official JCS positions have intrinsic political importance in the policy process as well. The JCS is the symbol and the statutory embodiment of the "military" viewpoint, and its official positions are widely regarded as the "military's" expert policy recommendations.[1] As a consequence, successive administrations have endeavored to secure the Chiefs' public support and, perhaps more importantly, to avoid their public disapproval.

As can be seen in table 4, the official record of the Joint Chiefs is overwhelmingly one of consensus: the proportion of "split" recommendations rarely exceeded 1 percent annually. The fact of this widespread consensus is significant and the implications will be explored below. It also means that split papers as a *percentage* of total recommendations never will be large and may be obscured by greater changes in the JCS workload. Accordingly, our analysis must be confined to a consideration of changes in the absolute number of JCS split positions.[2]

If the number of formal disagreements is taken as a measure of interservice rivalry, the data do not correspond to our image of the dozen years prior to U.S. involvement in Vietnam. The widely accepted description of the period from 1953 to 1969 is that the Eisenhower administration was characterized by relatively intense interservice rivalries and only modest civil-military tension, while the Kennedy and Johnson years saw a dramatic increase in civil-military conflict and a (corresponding) increase in interservice cooperation.[3] There were, however, an average of twice as many official JCS disagreements per year during the 1960s as during the 1950s. The disparity is even greater if attention is confined to the period preceding the Vietnam buildup.

Moreover, there is only partial support for the hypothesized relationships between the level of defense spending and the intensity of interservice rivalries. The hypothesis appears to be supported for the McNamara period when budget data for a fiscal year are associated with JCS recommendations for the preceding calendar year,

Table 4. Joint Chiefs of Staff Recommendations

Calendar Year	Total Recommendations	Divided Recommendations
1953	600	6
1954	700	7
1955	700	7
1956	965	6
1957	884	3
1958	887	13
1959	1,038	24
1960	1,066	21
1961	1,405	15
1962	1,458	13
1963	1,460	42
1964	1,593	47
1965	3,017	40
1966	3,281	7
1967	2,690	6
1968	2,575	6

Sources: 1953–57 data estimated from Huntington (1961a, p. 160). 1958–68 data supplied by Joint Staff.

as shown in table 5. In particular, the dramatic increase in the number of JCS splits approximately corresponded to a sharp cut in the annual budget increase in FY 1964 followed by actual reductions in the amount requested for defense in the next two years. Likewise, the reversal in the pattern of JCS dissension occurred at approximately the same time as the large budget increases which resulted from the Vietnam buildup.

However, no similar pattern can be constructed for the 1950s. There were very few split recommendations during the first two years of the Eisenhower administration when requests for defense appropriations were sharply reduced. During the four years of steady budget growth in FY 1956, the number of splits ranged from three to thirteen. These results suggest that the relationships between the level of defense spending and the dimensions and intensity of conflict may be somewhat more complex than the literature indicates.

JCS Decision-making: Incentives for Interservice Cooperation

The paucity of JCS splits is, in part, simply a reflection of the routine, noncontroversial business which generates the preponderance of formal JCS recommendations. Only the most important issues before the JCS are decided personally by the Chiefs (including all matters on which the services are unable to reach agreement). The remaining issues are processed through alternative decision-making mechanisms and delegations of authority. From 1958 to 1964, only about 25 percent of the formal JCS recommendations were personally decided by the Chiefs. With the introduction of an additional procedure for the handling of noncontroversial matters in 1965, the proportion of JCS decisions personally considered by the Chiefs declined to 5 percent (U.S., Blue Ribbon Defense Panel, Appendix N, p. 20).

There also are organizational pressures to achieve consensus on issues on which there is initial disagreement. The growing volume of JCS decisions increases the danger that the staffing machinery simply will break down under the load. Unanimous recommendations mitigate this problem since they take less time to process than do split positions.[4] Unanimous recommendations also create an atmosphere more conducive to coping with the workload by reducing conflict among the Chiefs and within the staff.

Most important, the services' bargaining advantages vis-à-vis the administration are enhanced to the extent that they are able to

Table 5. Comparison between JCS Split Recommendations and Annual Changes in Defense Budget Requests

Calendar Year	Number of Split Recommendations	% Change in Annual Budget Request	Defense Budget Request (× $1,000)	Fiscal Year
1953	6	—17.91	38,809,578	1954
1954	7	—20.60	30,814,142	1955
1955	7	8.44	33,414,955	1956
1956	6	7.93	36,063,330	1957
1957	3	7.23	38,670,724	1958
1958	13	7.43	41,543,280	1959
1959	24	2.18	42,450,484	1960
1960	21	— 3.73	40,825,023	1961
1961	15	2.86	41,994,345	1962
1962	13	18.99	49,967,646	1963
1963	42	2.26	51,280,384	1964
1964	47	— 3.76	49,349,752	1965
1965	40	— 4.35	47,201,107	1966
1966	7	24.58	58,804,063	1967
1967	6	26.24	74,236,736	1968
1968	6	5.73	78,491,902	1969

cooperate with one another and to adopt unanimous positions. Agreement among the services reduces the probability of civilian participation—"interference"—in the process of making recommendations concerning the use of military force: a divided JCS permits (or obliges) the administration to intervene to arrive at decisions when its military advisors cannot (Ginsburg 1964).[5]

In addition, unanimity among the Chiefs enhances their bargaining advantages by increasing the opportunity to exploit the image of military professionalism. A united stand connotes a disinterested expertise which is unsullied by partisanship—either political or service. Dissension among the military services threatens that image and makes claims to exclusive expertise more vulnerable. An administration confronted with divided military counsel can pick and choose among the menu of recommendations, assured of public support from at least some of the men in uniform (Lucas and Dawson 1974, p. 53).

Although it is undoubtedly true that the individual Chiefs would prefer to make recommendations which give enthusiastic support for the favorite programs of each, they seem prepared to go a long way toward compromising their preferences—or obscuring their differences—in order to reach "official" agreement. The Chiefs' behavior in this regard is consistent with *their* acceptance of the hypothesis that the extent of civilian participation (and control) is positively related to the intensity of interservice rivalries.

JCS Decision-making: Sources of Interservice Rivalry

Nevertheless, the Joint Chiefs sometimes cannot reach agreement among themselves: split papers do occur. The origins of this interservice rivalry are to be found in the stresses which afflict all complex organizations.

Several students of bureaucratic behavior have noted the importance of a stable, or at least predictable, environment for the coordination of large numbers of individuals over time (Cyert and March 1963, pp. 118–20). Organizations seek to reduce the uncertainty they confront by attempting to decrease their dependence on, and interaction with, other units (March and Simon 1958, p. 159; Kaufman 1971, p. 82). Given an irreducible interdependence among the military services, each service's efforts to stabilize its own organizational environment contain the seeds of unappeasable jurisdictional claims and insatiable demands for additional resources. In the absence of countervailing pressures, the interaction of these efforts will produce interservice rivalries over roles and missions as well as budget shares.

These pressures are reinforced by structurally related incentives to engage in bureaucratic self-promotion. Organizational specialization tends to limit interactions within, and especially among, the services. As a result, they—like the transient civilian policy-makers—tend to substitute organizational stereotypes and caricatures for rich and complex images of their counterparts' behavior (Jones 1973, pp. 146–47). Likewise, each service looking sideways is likely to share policy-makers' beliefs that the other services are parochial, rigid, and unresponsive. In view of the apparent limitations of its military competitors, each service—sincerely seeking loyally to serve the president—is inclined to recommend policies which increase its own role at the expense of the others. As William Jones (1973, p. 150) has observed:

Responsible officials feel powerfully moved to recommend *their* solutions. Each recommendation is likely to be related to the use of the organization controlled by the recommending official simply because that is the capability in which he has the greatest confidence.

In brief, the strong incentives for interservice consensus confront considerable pressure for interservice rivalry. As in the case of JCS unanimity, certain occasions for official disagreement are highly predictable. A service Chief will dissent, almost as a matter of routine, if the JCS is asked to endorse a position which threatens a core mission of that service: recommendations to reduce the number of Army divisions, the number of aircraft carriers, or the funding for the follow-on manned bomber have been virtual guarantees of a dissent from the service Chief affected. To remain effective in his role as chief of staff, he must seek the compliance of his subordinates. To maintain the morale and to stimulate the loyalty of these subordinates, the Chief must be prepared to cause a split paper, whatever his personal views and the pressures for JCS unanimity notwithstanding. Occasional dissents also perform another function: they credibly establish the agreement of a Chief as something that can be withheld. The Chief therefore can seek some concessions (however modest) in exchange for his vote.[6]

However, none of these pressures to provoke a formal JCS dissent is very sensitive to differences among civilian administrations. None yields much insight into the relationship between an administration's choices and the probability of disagreement among the Joint Chiefs. Our concern with the distribution of bargaining advantages among the participants requires that this relationship be understood.

Huntington relates the incidence of split recommendations to the presence of dependable administration support for a particular military service. He argues (1961a, p. 157) that a service's willingness to compromise within the JCS depends upon its predictions of the consequences for *itself* if the Chiefs are unable to present a unanimous recommendation to the politicians: the more confident a service is that its position will be supported when appealed to the president (or secretary of defense), the less willing it is to make concessions to the positions and interests of the other services.

Huntington's proposition entails a curious implication for interservice rivalry as a mechanism of civilian control. According to Huntington, unpredictable administration support—which might be thought to stimulate competition among the services—actually increases their incentives to achieve consensus. He advises instead that reliable administration support for a single service will enhance civilian control by provoking interservice rivalries. Testing this hypothesis therefore seems central to evaluating the performance of previous administrations and to constructing policy advice for their successors.

One common measure of the administration's relative treatment of the services is given by the composition of its defense budget requests to Congress. Service percentage shares of the president's annual defense budget are shown in table 6. These data document the well-known pattern of increasing Air Force dominance of the defense budget during the Eisenhower administration and a diminution of disparities between the services during the 1960s. In FY 1954, the Air Force received about one-third of the three-service budget. Its share quickly increased to more than 45 percent. In FY 1956, for example, growth in the Air Force budget exceeded the total annual increment and was financed from reductions in the budgets of the other two services.

However, an analysis of administration support based on the services' shares of the total annual defense budget exaggerates the president's budgetary discretion. A very large proportion of any annual defense budget is substantially immune to reallocation in the near term: year-to-year redistribution of resources can occur only at the margin. Accordingly, the data in table 6 obscure the allocation of *uncommitted* resources.

Table 6. Allocation of Presidential Defense Budget Request, by Service

Fiscal Year	Army	Navy	Air Force
(1954[a]	39.05%	27.57%	33.39%)
1955	28.04	33.71	38.25
1956	24.22	28.51	47.27
1957	23.19	30.01	46.80
1958	24.03	29.59	46.38
1959	23.73	29.03	47.23
1960	23.74	28.85	47.41
1961	24.29	30.57	45.14
(1962[a]	24.73	32.33	42.94)
1963	25.12	32.89	41.98
1964	26.80	31.82	41.39
1965	26.12	32.09	41.78
1966	26.00	32.73	41.27
1967	31.11	30.82	38.07
1968	33.92	30.34	35.73
1969	34.10	30.69	35.21

Note: The table is based on a three-service total, excluding OSD.
[a]Presidential transition years.

Table 7 represents an effort to respond to this problem. The difference between the president's total defense budget request in the current year and in the preceding year was computed as a gauge to budgetary flexibility. The between-year change in the president's budget request for each service was calculated as a percentage of this total change. Then the services were rank-ordered according to their percentage share of the annual budget increment (or decrement). The service receiving the largest proportion of the annual increment (or smallest share of the decrement) was coded=1, the middle service was coded=2, and so on. Thus, administration support for a service would be indicated by a higher ranking.

The results in table 6 also conceal the administration's changes in each service's annual budget estimate submitted to the secretary of defense. Although every service's estimate is reduced during the annual budget review within the administration, the *relative* size of that reduction is another indication of the extent of administration support. That support was calculated as the ratio of two proportions:

$$\text{Relative support} = \frac{(E_i - R_i)/(E_{tot} - R_{tot})}{(E_i / E_{tot})}$$

where:

$E_i =$ the annual budget estimate to the secretary submitted by service$_i$

$R_i =$ the amount included in the president's annual budget request to Congress for service$_i$

$E_{tot} =$ the sum of the annual service budget estimates submitted to the secretary

$R_{tot} =$ the total amount included in the president's annual budget request for the three services

The resulting ratio of these two proportions is a measure of each service's budget reduction relative to its request. The smaller the ratio, the less the relative reduction made by the administration.

The services were rank-ordered according to the magnitude of their relative reduction: the service receiving the smallest relative reduction was coded=1, and so on. These results are shown in table 8. A ratio of less than 1.0 indicates that the service's share of the total difference was less than its share of the sum of the service estimates. Rank-orderings reflecting values less than 1.0 are underlined in table 8.

Table 7. Services' Shares of Annual Budget Request Changes, Rank-Order

Fiscal Year	Army	Navy	Air Force	Fiscal Year	Army	Navy	Air Force
1955	3	1	2	1963	3	1	2
1956	2	3	1	1964	1	3	2
1957	3	1	2	1965	3	1	2
1958	2	3	1	1966	2	1	3
1959	2	3	1	1967	1	3	2
1960	3	2	1	1968	1	2	3
1961	2	1	3	1969	2	1	3

Note: 1 = largest share of annual budget increment or smallest budget decrement.

Summary: Sum of Annual Ranks

	1955–61	1963–69
Army	17	13
Navy	14	12
Air Force	11	17

Table 8. Relative Reduction in Services' Budget Estimates, Rank-Order

Fiscal Year	Army	Navy	Air Force	Fiscal Year	Army	Navy	Air Force
1955	3	1	2	1963	3	1	2
1956	2	3	1	1964	1	3	2
1957	1	3	2	1965	1	2	3
1958	3	1	2	1966	2	3	1
1959	2	1	3	1967	1	2	3
1960	3	2	1	1968	1	3	2
1961	3	1	2	1969	1	3	2

Note: 1 = Smallest relative reduction. Underlined ranks indicate less than proportional reduction.

Summary: Sum of Annual Ranks

	1955–61	1963–69
Army	17	10
Navy	12	17
Air Force	13	15

Both the across-time measures shown in table 7 and the within-year measures in table 8 further confirm the Eisenhower administration's support for the Air Force and that service's consequent budget growth. Table 7 shows that the Air Force garnered the largest budget increase increment in four of the seven Eisenhower years. During that period, it ranked about the same as the Navy in terms of relative share of budget reduction. By both measures, the Army suffered a consistent decline during the 1950s.

The budget data for the succeeding Democratic administration suggest that no service could depend upon the consistent support of the administration. During the four years prior to the Vietnam buildup (FY 1963 to FY 1966), each service suffered the most and the least in terms of relative share of the reduction from their combined budget estimates. Similarly, each service bore less than its "fair share" (i.e., the ratio was less than 1.0) in at least one of those years. The Army and the Navy each ranked both highest and lowest in their respective shares of the annual budget increment during the four-year period while the Air Force ranked in the middle in three of those years.

Inclusion of the Vietnam war years in the analysis conveys an impression of administration budgetary support for the Army. The data in table 8 suggest that the Army fared even better during the 1960s than the Air Force did during the Eisenhower administration. Indeed, it ranked first in five of the seven years. Each time, its share of the reduction in the total budget request was less than its budget share.

If Huntington's account is correct, this budgetary analysis would lead us to expect that the Eisenhower administration was characterized by a rash of JCS split decisions provoked by an Air Force assured of administration support. The pattern of administration (budgetary) support shifting among the services in the early 1960s would lead to the prediction of a decline in JCS split decisions during the pre-Vietnam period. Finally, we would predict a steady increase in the number of JCS split papers as the record of administration support for the Army was established and strengthened during the Vietnam buildup. These predictions, however, are almost exactly the *opposite* of the actual record of JCS split papers reported in table 4. Moreover, the available evidence suggests that the Army, rather than the Air Force, was the major dissenter during the Eisenhower administration while the Air Force caused the overwhelming proportion of split decisions during the early 1960s (Taylor 1960, pp. 107–8; interviews).

Disproportionate resource allocation per se nevertheless may be a *barrier* to interservice agreement: whether by design or by inadvertence, differential treatment of the military services by the administration may contribute to interservice rivalry. Some indication of budgetary discrimination is suggested by the magnitude of the disparity between the most favored and least favored military service.

This budgetary distance was computed in the following manner. The difference between the president's total defense budget request in a given year and congressional appropriations for the preceding year was calculated as a conservative estimate of discretionary resources (table 9, col. 1). The between-year change in the president's budget request for each service was calculated as a percentage of this total change (table 9, cols. 2–4). (Since OSD budget changes are included in the defense total, the service percentages do not sum to 100.) The difference between the largest and smallest percentage shares of the budget change was calculated as a measure of equality of treatment: results approximating zero indicate equal shares of the budget change; the larger the difference, the greater the disparity (table 9, col. 5).

The most dramatic examples of differential treatment are those years in which the *direction* of the budget change is not the same

Table 9. Allocation of Annual Budget Change, by Service
(President's Budget Request$_t$ — Congressional Appropriations$_{t-1}$)

| Fiscal Year | Total Change (× $1,000) | Percentage Allocation of Budget Change to Services | | | Maximum Difference (%) |
		Army	Navy	Air Force	
	(1)	(2)	(3)	(4)	(5)
(1954[a]	— 8,263,121.	17.32%	—31.64%	— 93.18%	110.50%)
1955	— 4,689,533.	—102.02	10.92	— 4.45	112.94
1956	3,204,532.	— 1.41	—23.74	120.32	144.06
1957	2,303,034.	18.73	41.57	40.24	22.84
1958	1,585,373.	63.06	32.65	1.38	61.68
1959	4,455,097.	33.54	19.18	34.30	15.12
1960	1,209,473.	30.11	0.19	66.52	66.33
1961	— 76,200.	b	b	b	b
(1962[a]	3,098,460.	29.71	48.57	16.77	31.80)
1963	1,887,343.	— 4.93	46.56	28.20	51.49
1964	1,543,476.	69.12	— 5.57	— 27.91	97.03
1965	544,100.	— 59.09	29.46	37.20	96.29
1966	— 1,121,919.	— 30.76	—20.95	— 76.53	55.58
1967	12,282,051.	47.84	24.46	25.29	23.38
1968	15,473,558.	41.03	26.98	24.98	16.05
1969	6,745,218.	32.94	37.41	25.23	12.18

[a]Presidential transition years.
[b]See text on FY 1961 calculations.

for all three services, that is, an increase over last year's appropriations is requested for one service while less than last year's appropriations is requested for another service. Such cases would seen to make reaching unanimous military recommendations on defense policy especially difficult. Accordingly, FY 1954 to 1956, 1961,[7] and 1963 to 1965 would be expected to be years in which it was most difficult to achieve consensus. Approximately the same magnitudes and, presumably, similar difficulties are indicated for FY 1958 and FY 1966. The time period which seemed most conducive to interservice agreement and consensus was during the large-scale American participation in Vietnam. From FY 1967 to 1969, the maximum percentage difference in service shares of the annual budget change steadily narrowed.

A comparison of these results and the record of JCS split recommendations reveals an approximate correspondence between differential budget treatment and JCS dissents during the Kennedy and Johnson years. The pre-Vietnam buildup period was characterized by disparate allocations of the annual budget change and an increase in the number of split papers. During U.S. involvement in Vietnam, a (substantially increased) budget increment was distributed more equally among the services, and the number of JCS split recommendations declined. These results from the 1960s suggest that it is less a matter of consistent administration support for a particular service provoking splits than a matter of unequal treatment per se inhibiting cooperation.

Data from the Eisenhower administration, however, run counter to the predictions. The entire period was characterized by a modest level of JCS splits (compared to the early 1960s). To the extent that there is a trend toward increasing JCS dissension, it is the opposite of the pattern of the allocation of annual budget changes. Very large disparities in the allocation of annual budget changes early in the Eisenhower administration corresponded to a low incidence of JCS splits. More equal budget treatment later in the administration was accompanied by an increase in the number of splits. Note especially that from FY 1955 to 1957, when the Army was receiving relatively harsh treatment, the number of JCS splits was at their lowest level.[8]

These data from the Eisenhower administration highlight the fact that disparate budget treatment of the services does not *force* JCS splits any more than equal treatment compels unanimity. Rather, roughly equal treatment *permits* or facilitates interservice agreement. Additional factors must be introduced to account for the pattern of split papers. Unanimous JCS recommendations imply a complementarity of interests among the Chiefs *and* the absence of any important obstacles to cooperation. Conversely, a split recommendation implies the absence of sufficiently complementary interests *and* an expected benefit to be derived from formal disagreement. The importance of this latter condition is highlighted by comparing Army and Air Force responses to similar conditions.

The position of the Air Force in the early 1960s resembled that of the Army during the Eisenhower administration: core activities of each service were being threatened with reduction or, in the extreme, elimination. Yet, during the period in which the threat was most salient to the Army, there were very few split papers emerging from the JCS. Ries (1964, p. 203) has remarked on "the Army's failure to challenge the defense budgets of 1954 and 1958. In each case its plight was worse and its case was better than that of the Navy in 1949, but there was no 'revolt of the generals.' " By contrast, the greatest number of dissents was recorded during the 1960s when the future of the manned bomber (although neither the survival of the Air Force as an organization nor as a flying service) was threatened.

A critical difference between the two time periods was the dearth of any important sources of support for the Army's case outside the executive branch during Eisenhower's first term compared to the loud and vociferous advocacy of the Air Force's case in the early 1960s. The Army had little incentive to break ranks and publicly complain when there were no external actors both able to help and inclined to be sympathetic. By contrast, the Air Force during the 1960s—fearing a loss within the executive branch—sought to expand the circle of participants by alerting and supporting outside allies.

Congress as an Ally

The constitutionally defined allocation of governmental responsibilities between Congress and the executive branch—which Neustadt (1960, p. 33) has aptly described as "separated institutions *sharing* powers"—makes Congress the most immediately influential source of support and opposition for both the president and the services. Administrations routinely seek the support of senior military officers in order to persuade Congress to approve their proposals and fund their programs. The military services frequently look to Congress to reverse or mitigate unfavorable decisions taken by the administration (Enthoven and Smith 1971, pp. 310–11).

This organizational untidiness of multiple lines of formal authority between politically accountable decision-makers and military officers has a standing in law as well as custom. Congress has traditionally—and successfully—demanded *direct* access to the "professional military advice" of the Joint Chiefs. For example, Congress insisted that the 1958 Reorganization Act include a provision which gave the military chiefs direct and unrestricted access to Congress with "any recommendations relating to the Department of Defense that they might deem proper" (quoted in Eisenhower 1965, p. 252).[9]

The military, in turn, have perceived an opportunity (and perhaps an obligation) to exploit the separation of powers. Earle Wheeler, while serving as chairman of the Joint Chiefs of Staff, observed (quoted in Powell 1967, pp. 47–48):

In answer to direct questions, the military leader has no moral alternative to giving Congress the same candid professional judgments that he had previously stated within the JCS, to the Secretary of Defense, or the President.

From this perspective, military "insubordination" to their civilian "superiors" in the executive branch is sanctioned (or demanded) by statute. Thus, Maxwell Taylor (1964, p. 337) declared in a speech he delivered as JCS chairman: "The officers have the *responsibility* of presenting their views to their civilian superiors *whether they are requested or not*" (emphasis added).[10]

These multiple authority relationships permit a service, in good conscience, to give less than full and faithful compliance with an administration decision, to impose the most congenial interpretation on an ambiguous order, to exercise professional military judgment, and to appeal to *other* superiors for a reversal of an offending directive. As a corollary, congressional preferences for a particular service and willingness to support its proposals (and its implementing budget requests) may help to account for the Chiefs' relative incentives to concede or dissent within the JCS.

The dominant feature of Eisenhower's "New Look" in defense policy was the substitution of firepower for manpower, with an emphasis on nuclear weapons and general war contingencies. As Eisenhower (1967, pp. 214–15) recalled:

Essentially, it [the New Look] was a decision to avoid primary dependence on numerical strength of military forces, as in the past, and to turn more to the sophisticated weapons then emerging—missiles, higher performance planes, nuclear weapons, and various other scientifically advanced systems—as the basis of military organization and planning.

At least until the late 1950s, Congress was enthusiastic about the prospects of substituting firepower for manpower and frequently appropriated more funds than the Eisenhower administration had requested.[11]

Congressional treatment of Eisenhower's budget requests provides an indication of its defense preferences. Particular budget categories reflect the distinction between manpower and firepower. A strategy which emphasizes ground combat and land warfare requires forces which would be provided primarily by the Army and, to a lesser extent, the Marine Corps. Congressional support for such a strategy, and the manpower required to implement it, would be reflected in the military personnel budgets for the Army and the

Marines. Congressional support for firepower should be reflected in its treatment of budget requests for procurement. A somewhat more refined indicator of congressional emphasis on a "firepower strategy" would exclude the procurement of equipment necessary for ground combat. Accordingly, congressional treatment of budget requests for Air Force aircraft procurement also was examined.[12]

In an effort to relate congressional action on each of these budget activities to congressional action on the total defense budget in a given year, the ratio of each category's percentage share of the total congressional reduction in the president's budget to that line item's proportion of the presidential budget request was computed.[13] Across-the-board congressional budget actions which did not distinguish among categories would yield ratios equal to 1.0. The results are shown in table 10. (Negative values in table 10 indicate congressional increases in the president's budget requests, that is, "negative budget cuts.")

Table 10. Congressional Funding of Personnel and Procurement, Ratio of Proportional Budget Change to Proportion of Budget Request

Fiscal Year	Army and Marine Military Personnel	Procurement, All Services	Air Force Aircraft Procurement
1954	0.09	1.91	3.66
1955	0.33	1.06	0.32
1956[a]	—11.53	1.30	— 3.87
1957[a]	— 0.19	—13.75	—25.94
1958[a]	1.44	1.31	0.69
1959[a]	— 2.82	—13.78	— 7.66
1960[a]	4.09	— 0.39	0.15
1961[a]	0.11	— 1.87	— 6.78

Note: Negative ratios indicate congressional increases in budget category.
[a]Congressional appropriations exceeded President's budget request.

These ratios indicate that Congress gave budget requests for procurement relatively more favorable treatment than requests for manpower during the Eisenhower administration. Specifically, the total procurement budget was increased relatively more (or decreased less) than the military personnel budget during each of the last five years of the Eisenhower administration. The same is true for Air Force aircraft procurement which also received a slight advantage in FY 1955. Only in FY 1954—the last Korean War budget and transitional Truman-Eisenhower budget—did Air Force aircraft procurement suffer a relatively large reduction. While hardly conclusive, these data are suggestive of congressional policy preferences during the 1950s: Congress gave enthusiastic budgetary support to a defense policy which emphasized Air Force responsibilities at the expense of Army capabilities.

A more direct indication of congressional support for each of the services, and one which does not address the more difficult area of divining congressional policy preferences, is the comparative fate of each service's annual budget request. Congressional behavior was measured in two related ways. First, annual congressional appropriations as a percentage of the administration request for each service was computed. This is a straightforward measure of which service(s) received more or less than the administration requested and permits simple comparisons among the services. These data are shown in table 11. A second measure of congressional treatment of the ser-

Table 11. Congressional Appropriations as Percentage of President's Budget Request

Fiscal Year	Army	Navy	Air Force	Total Defense Budget
1954	95.06%	96.97%	97.61%	88.25%
1955	92.79	98.06	95.67	96.11
1956	96.78	101.93	99.70	100.62
1957	97.14	99.52	105.06	100.67
1958	85.30	94.00	96.72	92.65
1959	102.45	105.87	102.34	99.10
1960	103.48	98.74	97.79	94.28
1961	100.77	102.19	100.27	102.82
1962	113.81	106.70	105.75	114.15
1963	98.88	98.36	101.85	100.53
1964	95.94	95.62	95.74	95.81
1965	97.39	98.45	98.26	98.39
1966	99.15	97.74	99.13	100.19
1967	100.95	100.04	100.39	100.25
1968	97.31	95.43	97.77	97.65
1969	94.27	91.07	94.31	93.05

Summary: 1954–61

Sum of Annual Ranks

Army	20
Navy	12
Air Force	15

vices is the ratio of a service's proportional share of the total congressional budget reduction (or increase) to its proportional share of the president's defense budget request. These results are shown in table 12.

Table 12. Congressional Funding of Service Budgets, Ratio of Proportional Budget Change to Proportion of Budget Request

Fiscal Year	Army		Navy		Air Force	
	Ratio	Rank	Ratio	Rank	Ratio	Rank
1954	1.18	3	0.73	2	0.57	1
1955	2.00	3	0.54	1	0.67	2
1956[a]	2.19	3	—1.31	1	0.20	2
1957[a]	0.91	3	0.15	2	—1.61	1
1958	2.19	3	0.89	2	0.49	1
1959[a]	—0.70	2	—1.67	1	—0.67	3
1960[a]	—1.60	1	0.58	2	1.01	3
1961[a]	—0.78	2	—2.21	1	—0.27	3
1962[a]	—1.68	1	—0.81	2	—0.70	3
1963[a]	0.69	2	1.02	3	—1.14	1
1964	0.95	1	1.03	3	1.00	2
1965	1.26	3	0.74	1	0.84	2
1966[a]	0.57	1	1.52	3	0.58	2
1967[a]	—2.09	1	—0.09	3	—0.86	2
1968	0.81	2	1.37	3	0.67	1
1969	0.88	2	1.37	3	0.87	1

Note: Negative ratios indicate Congressional increases in service budget.

[a]Congressional appropriations exceeded President's budget request.

Both measures reveal the same pattern of congressional actions: the Army's budget was treated the least favorably of any of the services until the late 1950s. In each of the first five years of the Eisenhower administration, Congress reduced the Army's budget more than that of the other two services. In two of the three years in which the Congress appropriated more funds for the Army than Eisenhower had requested, appropriations for the Navy and the Air Force also exceeded 100 percent. Only in FY 1960 did the Army rank ahead of the other two services. On the other hand, the Army paid for most of the congressional reductions in Eisenhower's budget requests in FY 1955 and FY 1958, as well as financed most of the additional appropriations voted for the Navy in FY 1956.

The modest increase in JCS split recommendations in the last years of the Eisenhower administration roughly corresponds to an increase in congressional support for the Army's budget (Lucas and Dawson 1974, p. 111). Although the Army was the service which was treated least favorably by Congress in FY 1959, even its appropriations exceeded the president's budget request. The following year, Congress increased the Army's budget over Eisenhower's request while simultaneously reducing the budgets of the other two services. In the last year of the Eisenhower administration, the Army shared congressional increases with the Navy while the Air Force's budget request was reduced for the second consecutive year.

In sum, the pattern of JCS split recommendations during the 1950s approximates the variations in congressional support for the service least favored by administration policy. To the extent that congressional support encourages dissent within the JCS, it is not surprising that the Army demurred as infrequently as it did during the 1950s. Unless and until there was some prospect of external support, there was little to be gained from such dissent, almost irrespective of how unfavorable the trend of defense policy was.

The contrast with the situation of the Air Force during the early 1960s is illuminating. All three services received large budget increases in the Kennedy administration's amendments to the FY 1962 budget and in its FY 1963 budget. In most cases, however, additional resources primarily were devoted to activities to which the services themselves assigned low priority. The Air Force in particular found that a large part of its budgetary increase had been earmarked for programs in which it had an only secondary interest, for example, airlift, nonnuclear ordnance (McNamara 1963).

The Air Force's core activities, by contrast, appeared to be threatened by Kennedy's budget choices. The conflict between the Kennedy administration and the Air Force—particularly over the future of the manned bomber—and the promise of congressional support for the service was previewed in the early months of the administration. In a handwritten note to Kennedy dated March 20, 1961, McNamara reported on the status of congressional increases in the President's amendments to the FY 1962 defense budget:

> We have utilized the funds for the purposes for which Congress appropriated them in 18 cases. Only in 3 cases—the B-52 [bomber] Wing; the B-70 [follow-on manned bomber]; and Dynasoar [piloted spacecraft]—have the funds been 'impounded by the Executive Branch.'

In 1963, the administration again denied additional funds for two Air Force programs—Skybolt and Dynasoar—which were central to the future of the manned bomber (York 1970, p. 63). The Air Force also was unable to get the administration to expand the B-70 bomber program beyond the two prototypes already approved. By that time, the Air Force was in a position roughly analogous to that of the Army under Eisenhower. Yet, in contrast to the Army, the Air Force elected to stand its ground in the JCS and to resist the pressures toward unanimity. The crucial difference may have been the congressional support available to the Air Force during this period.

In 1963, the manned bomber controversy was carried to Congress. Congressional efforts to expand the program, even to the point of raising a constitutional question if necessary, are well-known (Hunter 1973, pp. 192–94). The intensity of those efforts is perhaps best epitomized by Mendel Rivers's vow: "So help me God, we are going to have a follow-on bomber if it kills everyone in the Department of Defense, and I die in the process" (quoted in Roherty 1970, p. 103).

Aggregate budgetary evidence of congressional support for the Air Force during the 1960s is less clear than its lack of enthusiasm for the Army during the preceding decade. Indeed, the data in Table 11 suggest a picture of surprisingly *equal* treatment of the services by Congress beginning in FY 1964 and continuing through the Vietnam buildup in FY 1967.

The data in table 12 give modest additional indications of congressional support for the Air Force. That service ranked third among the services only once during the Kennedy-Johnson years. Even then, in FY 1962, ranking last meant that Congress *increased* appropriations for the Air Force over Kennedy's budget request. In the following year, Congress again exceeded the president's budget request for the Air Force while reducing the budget requests for the Army and the Navy. Most important, in no year during the Kennedy-Johnson administration did Congress reduce the Air Force budget in greater proportion than the reduction in the total defense budget.

At a minimum, the Air Force, unlike the Army in the 1950s, confronted no persistent congressional hostility. Moreover, extraordinary congressional support for some Air Force programs, most notably the follow-on manned bomber, gave strong indications of congressional sentiment. The Air Force Chief of Staff had a positive incentive to resist any JCS recommendation to reduce or abandon activities for which there might be support from external allies. The Air Force dissent alerted its congressional supporters to the issue. Moreover, those allies *needed* that dissent in order to continue the debate. If the Air Force Chief had agreed to a reduction, congressional efforts to carry on the battle might have appeared presumptuous, and perhaps a little foolish.

Conclusion

The pattern of JCS recommendations during the 1950s and 1960s is overwhelmingly one of consensus among the military services. This record of agreement reflects the services' mutual interest in restraining interservice rivalries. If civilian influence is (in part) a function of the intensity of interservice conflict, then the administration must create incentives which are sufficient to overcome the system's bias toward formal unanimity among the services.

The analysis of variations in the frequency of formal disagreements among the Joint Chiefs suggests some modifications in the propositions regarding interservice rivalries and in the policy advice derived from them. Huntington's explanation for split recommendations implies that administrations can increase competition among the military services by consistently and dependably favoring a single service. However, the analysis suggests a somewhat more complicated account which entails alternative policy advice. That is, the process usefully may be viewed as a combination of obstacles to interservice agreement and incentives for dissent.

Unequal budgetary treatment of the services by the administration appears to be one such obstacle. Indeed, the uncertainty spawned by unpredictable administration support might increase the barriers to interservice collusion. The incentives to dissent within the JCS appear to be related to the existence of supporters outside the administration—especially the Congress—who can influence the administration's decisions and actions. This aspect raises the broader questions of the administration's dependence upon the services for support and of the character of civil-military relations.

4

Interaction among Participants
Patterns of Military Support for Administration Policies

The president, like modern heads of government everywhere, is obliged to operate as the leader of large public bureaucracies. In virtually every area of foreign and domestic policy, he confronts large and complex tasks that must be divided into more manageable components and delegated to his nominal subordinates (March and Simon 1958; Simon, Smithburg, and Thompson 1970). From this standpoint, the characterization of the president as "chief executive" is particularly apt. His inescapable dependence on the bureaucracy requires him to address problems of coordination and integration, to inhibit the substitution of more parochial subgoals for his objectives, and to resist the diffusion of his resources of influence.

The president, in brief, is caught in a genuine paradox: he has no alternative but to delegate his responsibilities to others if he is to have any reasonable prospect of achieving his policy objectives. But that very requirement frequently spawns divergent purposes among his subordinates, provides them with the resources to counter his authority, and consequently reduces the probability that his goals will be fully and faithfully implemented (March and Simon 1958, pp. 152–53).

This paradox of delegation (Selznick 1949; Allison 1971, p. 80) is nowhere clearer than in the case of the president's relationship to the military services. The president has no choice but to delegate some of the responsibilities for national security to his uniformed subordinates; he cannot do it alone. The complexity of the tasks and the value of the stakes in national security policy, however, spawn obstacles which impede the realization of the president's national security preferences. His actions and choices are everywhere constrained by organizational dilemmas and political realities. The task confronting the president in his conduct of national security policy, therefore, is how to reduce the price he must pay in noncompliance to secure the cooperation of his nominal subordinates in uniform.

Organizational Constraints and Bureaucratic Politics: A Simple Typology of Noncompliance

Some distinctions among types of noncompliance will facilitate the analysis. "Compliance" connotes a congruence between the intentions of a superior in the organization and the behavior of his subordinates. "Noncompliance," of course, implies a discrepancy between the superior's purposes and the subordinates' actions.

The gap between intentions and actions depends on (a) the degree of goal congruence (or divergence) between superiors and subordinates, (b) the capabilities available to subordinates to accomplish their assignments, (c) the quality of communications between superiors and subordinates, and (d) the distribution of bargaining resources within the formal hierarchy.[1]

Some noncompliance is *unavoidable*: subordinates understand their superior's directives (and intentions) and are willing to work toward his goals (or are unable to resist his orders), but they, and the organizations of which they are members, lack the administrative capabilities or physical resources which are required. Robert Komer argues, for example, that however much the Kennedy administration believed that counterinsurgency was the appropriate military strategy in Vietnam, the Army *could not* comply: "the vast machinery, both human and technological, that *is* the U.S. Army is organized to implement a conventional strategy to the exclusion of a counterinsurgency/Vietnamization strategy" (quoted in Gallucci 1975, p. 386). That is, noncompliance is unavoidable when subordinates have been directed to undertake a task which is administratively or physically "impossible."

Another fraction of the noncompliance which occurs can be accounted for by honest confusion and misunderstanding. Subordinates may control the necessary organizational and physical resources and may be willing (or unable to avoid) faithfully implementing their superior's decisions. However, directives frequently are vague and confusing, appear to contradict previous orders, or omit the context which specifies the superior's intentions (Cronin 1970, p. 584). Subordinates in every organization are obliged to exercise some discretion: to make interpretations of, and to draw inferences from, directives. Accordingly, it is reasonable to anticipate circumstances in which the subordinate—acting in good faith —fails to divine his superior's intentions, and behaves contrary to the latter's wishes. During the early phases of the U.S. buildup in Vietnam, for example, it is at least plausible that the Joint Chiefs genuinely—if mistakenly—believed that the Johnson administration had endorsed their recommendation for large U.S. ground forces and an offensive strategy (Gallucci 1975, p. 386). Such behavior might be characterized as *inadvertent* noncompliance.[2]

Both inadvertent and unavoidable noncompliance assume subordinates who, for one reason or another, are motivated to implement the superior's decisions. However, it is easy to imagine a situation in which the subordinate understood and was capable of doing the bidding of the superior but nevertheless defied the latter's directives. Korb reports (1976, p. 162), for example, that when Lyndon Johnson approved an increase in U.S. *support* forces in early 1965, the JCS "ordered in . . . the 173rd Airborne Brigade, one of the Army's crack *combat* outfits" (emphasis added). Such behavior might be termed *deliberate* noncompliance.[3]

Deliberate noncompliance is the most intriguing—and troubling—type. The product of neither individual misunderstanding nor organizational shortcomings, it cannot be remedied by improved analysis, better people, or bureaucratic restructuring. Deliberate noncompliance not only presumes subordinates who have priorities which diverge from those of their superior but, more important, that they are able to choose and behave in terms of their own preferences. Under these conditions, only bargaining can ameliorate the problems of organizational control (March and Simon 1958, pp. 129–30).

To the extent that his policy choices depend upon the threat or use of violence, therefore, the president routinely will be confronted with situations in which he either can forego utilization of the military instrument, try to command reluctant compliance by a heavy investment of time and prestige, or bargain with his uniformed subordinates. As a result, negotiations and accommodations have marked the relationship between the politicians and the soldiers during both Republican and Democratic administrations.

Improving Military Compliance: Civil-Military Bargaining

It perhaps is surprising that the secretary who is alleged to have worked a "revolution" in the Pentagon with the strong and unwavering support of the Kennedy White House felt compelled to seek the support of—and to grant concessions to—the Joint Chiefs. It is even more surprising that Eisenhower, who "was regarded by virtually everyone as the nation's foremost military hero and military expert" (Legere and Davis 1969a, p. 175), actively solicited the support of the JCS and took deliberate measures to increase the chances that the endorsement would be forthcoming. Nevertheless, several students of the period have noted presidents' willingness to trade concessions on policy for military endorsement (Halperin 1972b; Snyder 1962).

For example, early in the Eisenhower administration, the JCS was unable to agree to an allocation of manpower within the ceiling imposed by the administration. When Secretary of Defense Wilson was informed by the Chiefs that agreement would be forthcoming if an additional 65,000 men were authorized, he agreed to the change, and the support of the JCS was secured (Snyder 1962, p. 442).

McNamara also solicited the support of the Chiefs for the administration's defense programs and, like Eisenhower, was prepared to make certain concessions (e.g., compromising on the number of B-52 bombers) to secure their public approval. Thus, he sought a statement of support from the JCS which could be included in his presentation of the FY 1966 budget to Congress. In a December 2, 1964, memorandum to the chairman, McNamara wrote:

> I believe that in major respects the proposed force structure reflects the views of a majority of the Chiefs. Therefore I should like to include a statement similar to the following in the letter by which I transmit the FY 1966 Budget to the President.

There followed a carefully hedged statement of JCS endorsement. McNamara's memorandum concluded: "Please let me know by December 8 whether such a statement is agreeable to the Chiefs."

The chairman's response to McNamara's request is not available. Nevertheless, a comparison of successive drafts of McNamara's budget letter to the president, which reveals several changes in the language of the JCS endorsement he had solicited, provides some clues. In particular, the final version included new language implicitly acknowledging that the secretary had rejected certain changes which had been recommended unanimously by the JCS and contained a weaker characterization of the adequacy of the forces which were being funded. The resulting statement of JCS support, which was repeated in substance during McNamara's congressional testimony (U.S. Congress, House, 1965 part III, p. 147) is worth quoting at length:

> In developing the program and reviewing the budget proposals, I have had the continuing counsel and assistance of the Joint Chiefs of Staff. Although the force structure does not include all the forces or force modernizations recommended by the Joint Chiefs or individual members thereof, the Joint Chiefs of Staff agree that the program supported by this budget will increase our over-all combat effectiveness and will provide effective forces in

a high state of readiness for defense of the vital interests of the United States.[4]

Another example of the concessions that McNamara was prepared to make to the Joint Chiefs occurred early in the Kennedy administration. In testimony regarding the consolidation of the separate intelligence capabilities of the individual services into the Defense Intelligence Agency (DIA), McNamara noted that the consolidation had the "complete support" and "concurrence" of the Joint Chiefs. The secretary went on to explain the reasons for the Joint Chiefs' endorsement:

> One of the reasons, of course, is that we propose that this new Agency operate under the direction of the Joint Chiefs of Staff *so they will have full opportunities to shape its operation.* [U.S. Congress, Senate, 1961 Part I, p. 1223; emphasis added][5]

While it is unsurprising that successive administrations were more than indifferent about securing endorsements from their senior military officers, it is worth emphasizing that these administrations thought enough of the services' support to pay some price for it. This leads to a consideration of the circumstances which substitute negotiations for command and the more interesting issue of the determination of the point at which the participants are unable to agree on a "price."

Civil-Military Bargaining: Mutual Dependence and Conflicting Incentives

As the previous chapter noted, the administration finds military support useful in strengthening its case before its domestic, and especially congressional, constituencies. To the extent that the services publicly support the administration's defense programs, the political risks and burdens of administration policy choices are diffused, and the attacks of domestic political critics are constrained (Hammond 1968, p. 60). These civilian incentives create some dependence upon the military and permit the services to press for concessions.

The utility of public support from the services—as well as the consequences of their opposition—depends upon the appearance of professional integrity: the military's opinion is valued by Congress and the electorate, and their support is sought by the incumbent administration, because of "their prestige, nonpartisan status, professionalism, and limited identity with the incumbent administration" (Hammond 1968, p. 60). That image threatens the administration if the military stands in opposition, but it also is the basis of the political support which the services can offer. Accordingly, the administration must tread lightly as it maneuvers for the military's endorsement lest that resource be demeaned. The military, for its part, must take care to preserve its image so that its support is valued by the administration and its opposition is feared: when senior officers appear to be loyal, but uncritical, administration spokesmen, their political value is sharply diminished. As Senator Taft explained when he called for the replacement of Truman's military chiefs: "I have come to the point where I do not accept them as experts" (quoted in Korb 1976, p. 103).

This creates something of a dilemma for the president. The administration must select those military spokesmen who are expected to be most sympathetic with its policy preferences but must do so in such a way as to not impugn their nonpartisanship and professionalism. That is, the support which is desired can be *solicited* only at some risk and with some vulnerability. This need to avoid the appearance of endorsements coming from military spokesmen for a particular group of incumbent politicians confers bargaining advantages upon those uniformed experts.

Not only does the president seek to minimize his vulnerability to opposition arising from his external constituencies, but he also has a complementary interest in reducing his vulnerability to attacks and resistance from his uniformed subordinates. When the services assume some of responsibility for the shape of the defense program, they have compromised themselves and are less effective in expressing opposition to the national security policies which emerge (Halperin 1972b, pp. 320–22).

Having at least some part of the military assume a portion of the responsibility reduces the administration's vulnerability in at least two ways. First, it reduces the number of decisions for which the administration must bear the responsibility (in the eyes of the military) and suffer the consequences (especially in terms of increased resentment and decreased willingness to voluntarily comply). Second, as Chapter 3 discussed, it reduces the bargaining advantages of the military by inhibiting any tendency for a united stand in opposition to the politicians. The services have less credibility as disinterested experts when they cannot agree among themselves; the administration can exploit divisions within the military, picking and choosing among the advocates of the various positions.

The administration's search for political support from the military therefore is undertaken with some ambivalence. On the one hand, the president would prefer to command rather than bargain with—and make concessions to—his military subordinates. On the other hand, such hierarchical negotiations promise the virtue of reduced opposition from the services, and decreased vulnerability to attacks from external critics of his defense policies. The tension between the two objectives helps to account for the uncertainty in calculating the acceptable price for such support and the variability of the outcomes.[6]

The services confront similarly conflicting incentives. In addition to a sense of professional obligation to advise their political superiors and abide by the final decision, cooperative participation in the process is likely to yield outcomes more favorable to the services than nonparticipation: the concessions extracted may be worth the support given in exchange. But, as Hammond argues (1968, p. 60), the military also have strong incentives to limit sharing the political responsibilities of the administration:

> Not all wanted resources will be granted anyway, and, if necessary, risks can always be assumed later, when the gains as well as the risks are more certain. Whether or not they have carried the political burden in peacetime, the military can be expected to reap the benefits of political risk-bearing in times of high national security threat anyway. To the extent that they understand this, military authorities are discouraged by their understanding from assuming political burdens in peacetime.

The interaction of these sets of conflicting incentives finds the politicians ambivalently and inconsistently seeking the political support of the services and the military attempting to shift the burdens back to the administration or avoid them altogether. The outcomes likely appear to the outside observer (or foreign government) to be at least inconsistent, and perhaps irrational.

Hierarchical Bargaining in the Pentagon
The distribution of bargaining advantages among the participants cannot be rigorously assessed. Nevertheless, it is possible to describe those advantages and to speculate about the interaction among the participants and the outcomes which result under ceteris paribus assumptions.

The president's most visible bargaining advantage is his formal authority. No one doubts his *right* to reject the recommendations of his military advisors, whether divergent or unanimous. Consequently, the Chiefs may hope to embarrass—and thereby to pressure—the administration, but they cannot overrule it. One facet of his authority, of course, is the president's access to a broad range of positive and negative sanctions which he can confer and inflict. These permit him to reward good performance, punish deviance, and otherwise exploit the services' incentives in order to encourage their support and compliance. As Neustadt's classic analysis (1960) has shown, however, the president's impressive array of formal powers does not result in his independence from his nominal subordinates. Although it is obvious that they need him, this should not obscure the fact that he also depends on them.

The services' bargaining advantages largely derive from their expertise in, and monopoly control of, the instruments of force and violence (Lucas and Dawson 1974, pp. 86–87). Although there is some overlap among their capabilities, each service is a "monopoly supplier" of most of the tasks it can perform (Wilensky 1967, pp. 29–31).[7] Consequently, a choice of military policy instruments ordinarily entails a choice of military agents. The utility of a military instrument substantially depends on the willingness of its provider to support the policy.[8] The service accordingly can invoke the unvoiced threat to delay, foot-drag, and foul-up as well as give the implicit assurance of competent, faithful, and expeditious implementation. To the extent that the services can agree among themselves, they can increase their mutual bargaining advantages by further reducing the alternatives available to the administration and by enhancing their image of nonpartisan professionalism.

The president and the services thus stand in a relationship of mutual, if unequal, dependence. His formal authority surely is not irrelevant, but neither is it sufficient. He cannot rely solely upon coercion because the services can engage in resistance and retribution. The one-way flow of sanctions in principle is replaced by the two-way flow of rewards and punishments in practice. The result is *bargaining* (Lindblom 1955).

It is not bargaining among equals nor is the organizational context within which it occurs irrelevant. On the contrary, the organizational structure and the formal hierarchy are central in determining the result of the interactions: relations between the president and the services are characterized by *hierarchical bargaining* (Hammond 1968, p. 57). The organizational outcomes will be a function of the distribution of bargaining advantages among the participants, as well as of their skill and will in utilizing them.

The president's formal authority is substantially immune to manipulation by the services. For most purposes, so too is the services' monopoly of expertise, and especially of the means of implementation. The most manipulable factor in the bargaining relationship is the impact of official disagreement among the Joint Chiefs.

From the perspective of the administration, unanimous support by the Joint Chiefs (within limits) is ideal, dependable acquiescence is tolerable, splits may be exploitable; but the unanimous opposition of the Joint Chiefs is to be avoided and can be successfully weathered only if infrequently confronted. The Chiefs, as we have seen, have a strong interest in unanimity per se. Consequently, to the extent that the president can influence the incentives within the JCS for dissent, he can reduce the probability of unanimous opposition.

Ordinarily, the president can expect to attract at least some votes in the JCS. First, the locus of formal authority and the reinforcing norms create such a presumption. Second, presidential appointees, especially the chairman, are customary—if unreliable—allies. Finally, because most defense programs distribute costs and benefits unequally among the services, at least those services which benefit from a program are inclined to support the president on it.

It follows that the Chiefs' incentives to reach agreement among themselves are accompanied by substantial barriers to reaching a unanimous position in *opposition* to the administration's preferences. Ordinarily, the maximum outcome a disadvantaged service can achieve is a split paper. Since a split recommendation usually is more acceptable to the politicians than to the military, the dissenting service is likely to join its sisters in support of the administration. Because both the politicians and the other services prefer unanimity to dissension, the dissenting service may be able to extract some concession as the price for its acquiescent support of administration policy.

If this description is approximately correct, it would account for the low incidence of split papers, and predict that the overwhelming proportion of unanimous recommendations are accepted by the administration.[9] Moreover, it suggests that while all the participants have incentives to negotiate, the normal distribution of bargaining advantages permits the civilians to make only limited concessions in order to secure the Chiefs' endorsement. Thus, in the examples of civil-military bargaining cited above, Eisenhower increased his manpower ceiling by about 3 percent to win the Chiefs' support. McNamara, who was more concerned about having to deal with conflicting intelligence reports—none of which he trusted—than with improving the quality of military intelligence—which he despaired of—gave control of the DIA to the Chiefs, and then proceeded to virtually ignore it.

Unanimous JCS opposition to the administration, accordingly, is an extraordinary event which requires an unusual combination of circumstances. In particular, the obstacles to interservice cooperation must be limited while the administration's need for military support increases. As shown in the previous chapter, the Eisenhower administration rarely confronted such a situation and it almost never found itself in the position of rejecting unanimous JCS recommendations: Maxwell Taylor reports (1960, pp. 91, 106) that only four such occasions occurred during the period from October 1955 to March 1959.

The successor Democratic administrations rejected somewhat more JCS positions. Early in the Kennedy administration, McNamara did not accept unanimous JCS recommendations to sharply increase funding in the FY 1963 budget for Army procurement and to maintain naval forces at the level reached during the Berlin buildup (McNamara 1961). These two early rejections may have been the acts of a new secretary of defense who was determined to demonstrate his willingness to challenge professional military advice and who had strong support from Kennedy, and in Congress (Kanter 1972).

Although the complete data are not available, it appears that McNamara rejected an increasing number of unified JCS positions beginning in the mid 1960s. Five unanimous recommendations relating to the FY 1966 budget were not accepted. The affected programs included each service's highest-priority programs: a new manned bomber, a new interceptor, surface-to-air missiles for bomber defense, ABM development, and nuclear attack submarines. Although the available records are not entirely clear, it appears that an additional five recommendations concerning the FY 1966 budget also were rejected or substantially modified by the secretary (McNamara 1964).[10]

The services increasingly challenged the secretary in the context of the annual budget cycle during the Vietnam War. McNamara's instructions for the preparation of the wartime budgets made it clear that he had an intense desire to control expenditures, both by conservative financial planning factors—which assumed the war would not continue beyond the current fiscal year—and by ordering the deferment or elimination of non-Vietnam-related programs. The budget guidance memorandum (U.S. Department of Defense 1966) for preparing the FY 1968 budget is illustrative:

Support for all forces beyond June 30, 1968 will be programmed at peacetime activity levels. The FY 1968 budget will not include amounts necessary to protect reorder leadtime at combat rates should hostilities continue into FY 1969.

It also ordered that:

Programs that are not urgent military requirements will be reduced to the lowest possible level of operation, deferred to later years, or deleted as appropriate to the character of the activity.

Notwithstanding these instructions, service budget estimates to the secretary increased faster than the president's steeply climbing budget requests to Congress. Service estimates exceeded the final budget document by 5 to 15 percent in the years prior to the Vietnam buildup. In each of the Vietnam War years, however, service budget estimates were more than 20 percent greater than the budget presented to Congress. Perhaps more significant in view of the explicit budget instructions, the services continued to request funds for their favorite weapons systems, which were unrelated to the Vietnam War: ABM, follow-on manned bomber, and nuclear attack submarines (Korb 1970).

McNamara's increasing rejection of unanimous JCS recommendations roughly coincides with the sharp decline in number of formal disagreements among the Chiefs beginning in 1966. Several events during this period help to account for the change in JCS voting patterns. In part, the Chiefs learned from bitter experience that, when they were unable to reach agreement, McNamara was more inclined to exercise his own judgment. As Forrest Frank notes (1975, p. 319):

to preserve their influence, the Joint Chiefs found it necessary to develop standard procedures for avoiding internal disagreement. Among these was deferral to the service or agency involved when only its programs or operations were concerned. . . . Budgetary matters were handled in the same way: no service would criticize the proposals of the other services unless those proposals were extremely costly.

The departure of two controversial personalities, Maxwell Taylor and Curtis LeMay, also advanced the cause of interservice harmony. Moreover, Taylor's successor as chairman, Earle Wheeler, simply refused to report many JCS splits to McNamara (Korb 1976, pp. 115–16).

Perhaps most important, the American buildup in Vietnam that had begun the previous year had culminated in full-scale, intense combat operations during 1966. In such circumstances the military's expertise, both actual and perceived, was at a premium (Hammond 1968, p. 60; Halperin 1972b, p. 318). Prior to Vietnam, McNamara may have appeared to have been politically invincible. He had fought and won several hard battles with the services and never lost the support of the White House. Even unanimous opposition seemed futile.[11]

However, with American troops in the field and firing their weapons, the military's prestige—and political influence—increased. As the conflict continued and intensified, and as McNamara's public enthusiasm for the strategy diminished, there was "growing evidence that McNamara's power and influence were in serious decline" (Hoopes 1969, p. 83). The president increasingly tended to choose the advice of his senior military officers over the recommendations of his secretary of defense. McNamara no longer seemed invincible.

If opposition to the secretary had a greater probability of success than previously, other conditions increased the chances that such opposition would be unanimous. As indicated in tables 6 and 9, the distribution of budget increments became more equal and service budget shares converged as the war progressed. Such evenhanded treatment removed one obstacle to interservice cooperation and reduced the administration's opportunities to co-opt some of the participants or to provoke splits. As will be seen below, these incentives were reinforced by a budget system whose procedures suppressed allocational rivalries.

Time and the Vietnam War also constrained the administration's ability to indulge any of the services. Because of the pressures to minimize the budget impact of the conflict, a part of its cost was financed out of the services' base-line forces, that is, those programs, activities, and forces which the services could reasonably have expected to be supported in peacetime. The 50 percent increase in defense spending between FY 1964 and FY 1968 therefore is somewhat misleading. Of the $75.9 billion defense budget in FY 1968, approximately $23 billion resulted from the incremental costs of Vietnam. Accordingly, non-Vietnam defense spending had increased by only $2 billion in four years. In constant dollars, this represented a *decline* of nearly 2 percent. By contrast, in constant dollars, the FY 1964 budget was 9 percent more than the FY 1961 budget.[12] This budget stringency promoted the alienation of all three services and reduced the chances of making any of them an ally.

The situation was aggravated by non-Vietnam budget pressures which increased throughout McNamara's tenure. McNamara postponed decisions about—and conflict over—many of the services' high-priority programs by confining them to the relatively low-cost research and development (R&D) stage. During the FY 1966 budget cycle, for example, he responded to unanimous JCS recommendations to procure several major weapons systems (e.g., manned bomber, new interceptor, ABM) by continuing them in R&D (McNamara 1964). However, projects cannot be held in an R&D status indefinitely: as development progresses, decisions about eventual production become unavoidable. Accordingly, every year that McNamara extended the R&D phase of a program, the effectiveness of the tactic was reduced.

The secretary's problem is suggested by table 13, which shows the percentage of the annual budget request devoted to procurement and to research and development.[13] The Kennedy administration continued the increased budget allocation for research and development which began late in the Eisenhower administration. However, the proportion of the budget devoted to procurement—which includes the production of successful R&D programs—*declined* steadily until large-scale American involvement in Vietnam. The modest increases for procurement which occurred during Vietnam included large amounts for the replacement of war losses. Thus, by the time of the Vietnam buildup, four years into McNamara's term, programs that had been generated by the substantial R&D budget increasingly required decisions either approving procurement or requiring cancellation. If McNamara were to agree to support a new weapons program of any service—for whatever reason—it would have entailed very large expenditures at precisely the time that the resources were least available.

Table 13. Procurement and RDT & E as Percentage of Total Defense Budget Request

Fiscal Year	Procurement	RDT & E	Fiscal Year	Procurement	RDT & E
1954	28.12%	10.54%	1962	29.75	12.31
1955	22.99	7.59	1963	33.22	13.82
1956	26.53	8.90	1964	32.97	14.35
1957	26.90	9.62	1965	28.23	13.83
1958	27.96	8.78	1966	24.51	14.45
1959	28.39	15.36	1967	28.32	11.94
1960	29.08	14.69	1968	31.40	9.99
1961	29.56	12.29	1969	30.11	10.37

In sum, the convergence of a number of factors during the last part of McNamara's tenure helps to account for the apparently increased frequency of unanimous military opposition to administration defense choices. Increasing resource contraints on non-Vietnam-related programs provided additional occasions for disagreement and conflict between the military and the administration. Simultaneously, approximately equal budgetary treatment of the services by the administration reduced the barriers to interservice consensus within the Joint Chiefs of Staff. Finally, the growing domestic political prestige of the military during the early years of the Vietnam War (accompanied by McNamara's decline) increased the services' bargaining advantages and the benefits of opposing the administration's policy positions.

Conclusion

The analysis suggests that changes in the level and allocation of resources can influence the probabilities of interservice agreement. By implication, the civilian administration can manipulate the services' bargaining advantages and the probabilities of deliberate noncompliance to the extent that it can adjust the patterns of funding.[14]

If the interactions among participants and their incentives can be influenced by changes in the level of resources, it seems reasonable to suppose that the organizational mechanisms and rules for resource allocation also can influence behavior. This appears to have been the foundation for the changes which Secretary of Defense McNamara introduced into the Defense Department. The McNamara Revolution was, at its heart, an assault on defense management during the Eisenhower administration. Its symbol and its procedural core was the Planning-Programming-Budgeting System (PPBS), a new method for resource planning and for budgeting. Its objectives included remedying the perceived deficiencies in the quality of decisions made during the Eisenhower years and increasing the probabilities of faithful compliance. The budgeting system was to be the vehicle for these reforms.

The purposes of PPBS thus derive from an understanding of the potential of the budget cycle and the budgeting mechanism as policy instruments. We therefore turn to a consideration of the expectations which informed the McNamara Revolution and to an evaluation of the impact of the budgeting system on behavior.

Budget-making as Policy-making
The Intended Consequences

Not only do budget data yield a useful picture of national security policy, but the formal rules for allocating resources—the budgeting system—may be viewed as a mechanism by which the administration can shape and manage the substance of that policy. The changes in the budgeting procedures and rules introduced during McNamara's tenure, the Planning-Programming-Budgeting System (PPBS), were based on an enthusiastic endorsement of both propositions. PPBS was to yield better decisions as well as outcomes in greater congruence with those decisions.[1]

The major criticism of the Eisenhower years was that the political leadership had failed to exploit the budgeting system as a means by which to achieve a coherent and coordinated defense program. The custodians of PPBS argued that the Eisenhower administration had exercised purely fiscal control, that is, control over the level of spending: "defense budgets represented essentially predetermined, arbitrary ceilings in the sense that they did not follow from decisions about strategy, military needs, and weapons systems"[2] (Enthoven and Smith 1971, p. 13). Eisenhower, it was implied, was concerned about *how much* was spent but exercised minimal control over *what* was bought.

In the view of its critics, the Eisenhower administration had abdicated its opportunity to control defense policy through defense spending. According to Alain Enthoven, Assistant Secretary of Defense for Systems Analysis (Enthoven and Smith 1971, p. 11):

> The Defense budget [during the Eisenhower administration] was far from being the vital policy instrument it should have been. Rather than a mechanism for integrating strategy, forces, and costs, it was essentially a bookkeeping device for dividing funds between the services and accounts and a blunt instrument for keeping a lid on defense spending.

Under such a budgeting system, defense planning became the responsibility of the military services by default. Charles Hitch (Defense Department Comptroller from 1961 to 1965) argued that during the Eisenhower administration: "Each service tended to exercise its own priorities" (1965, p. 24). He portrayed the strategic plans which resulted from this system as "essentially a pasting together of unilaterally developed service programs" (quoted in Roherty 1970, p. 79).

In the view of the PPBS advocates, Eisenhower's failure to exercise policy control through the defense budget was due less to negligence or unwillingness than to inability. The problem lay not only with the men who managed the Pentagon during the 1950s but with their management techniques. Hitch insisted (1965, p. 18): "The Defense Secretaries [who preceded McNamara] used this method [of arbitrary budget ceilings] because they lacked the *management techniques* needed to do it any other way" (emphasis added).[3] It followed that the perceived shortcomings could not be remedied merely by installing a secretary of defense who possessed a more dynamic definition of his job: even people with the role definitions and objectives of McNamara and his colleagues would have been paralyzed and stymied by the policy instruments used during the Eisenhower administration. Accordingly, the success of their intended reforms would depend in large measure on the consequences of the new formal system for resource allocation.

McNamara's Reforms: The Planning-Programming-Budgeting System

The incoming Kennedy administration immediately set about remedying the perceived deficiencies of the Eisenhower budget procedures. The overriding objective of PPBS was to integrate strategic planning and defense budgeting and to place the operation firmly under the control of the administration. A more powerful and more subtle system would replace the fiscal controls of the Eisenhower years: there were to be no predetermined ceilings on defense spending.[4]

Most important, the inevitable policy disputes among the services and civilians were to occur during the planning and programming phases of the annual budget cycle, prior to the services' preparation of their budget estimates. The outcomes of these conflicts were to be recorded as changes in the Five Year Defense Program (FYDP). The services' budget estimates then were to be derived from the FYDP rather than squeezed into a predetermined budget ceiling.[5] The previously hectic budget "crunch" (beginning in October when the services submitted their budget estimates to the secretary and ending in January with the president's budget message to Congress) would end. In its place would be an unhurried and essentially technical review of the procedures and assumptions used to estimate the budget-year costs of the previously approved programs. As

Hitch predicted in testimony before the Jackson Subcommittee (U.S. Congress, Senate, 1961, Part I, p. 1009):

> There should be no need for a hectic and hurried *program* review crammed into a few weeks in the midst of the annual *budget* review. This basic program review will have been accomplished and only a final check and some last minute adjustments should be needed as far as the programs are concerned. [Emphasis added]

The issue of the timing of the civilian intervention into the budget cycle is important because it reflects several of the diagnosed shortcomings of the Eisenhower administration system. According to this analysis, civilian decisions regarding defense programs prior to 1961 were generated as a virtual by-product of efforts to reconcile the services' budget estimates with the budget ceiling. Enthoven and Smith wrote (1971, p. 15): "The main concern of the Secretary of Defense and his staff [during the Eisenhower administration] was with cutting the service requests to fit predetermined budget limits." Defense *program* choices emerged as a consequence of defense *budget* decisions taken during the frenzied October to January budget crunch. Hitch testified (U.S. Congress, Senate, 1961, Part I, p. 1030): "a great many individual but very important program or weapon system decisions have been made in the past during the period of the budgetary review, and that budgetary review has not been focused on missions."

In brief, Hitch argued that his predecessors made decisions regarding military missions at the wrong time in the budget cycle and with the information cast in an inappropriate form. It was symptomatic of Eisenhower's failure to exploit the budget system as an instrument of policy control. The transformation of the October-to-January budget review into a bookkeeping exercise symbolized the changes which were to be wrought by PPBS. Under McNamara's leadership, there were to be no predetermined budget limits, decisions were to be made about defense *programs* rather than *budgets*, and the budget season was to be a technical review exercise rather than a crash effort to reduce spending.

Our budget data permit an evaluation of two related assertions. First, the data can be confronted with the predictions of several models of budget-cutting behavior which are consistent with the McNamara description of the Eisenhower system. Second, data from the two time periods can be compared in order to gauge the contrasts implied by that description.

Eisenhower as a Budget Cutter

The Eisenhower administration has been portrayed as one which set strict limits on total defense spending but granted considerable discretion to the military services to establish program priorities and to allocate resources. Some students of defense policy have argued that, in such circumstances, the most likely form of inter-service agreement is one premised on equal budget shares. For example, Crecine predicts (1969, p. 16): "A budgetary process which gives DOD a fixed amount for a given fiscal year and allows substantial freedom in its expenditure is likely to produce nearly equal service shares." However, the data in table 6 indicate a considerable disparity among the services' shares of the total defense budget during the Eisenhower administration. These data require us either to reject the hypothesis or to question the description of the Eisenhower budget system.

Even if the Eisenhower administration primarily had been concerned with the fiscal consequences of the annual defense budget, its role was not (or could not be) confined to promulgating budget ceilings within which the services were free to choose: if Eisenhower did impose budget ceilings prior to the services' preparation of their budget estimates, they were not observed.[6] As can be seen in table 14, the services' budgets always substantially exceeded the spending limits set by the president. Thus, the Eisenhower administration had considerable work to do *after* the services submitted their budget estimates each year.

Given the apparent failure of the Eisenhower administration's "ceilings" to limit the services' budget estimates, the PPBS diagnosis predicts that Eisenhower would seek to achieve his dominant

Table 14. President's January Budget Request as a Percentage of the Services' October Budget Estimates

Fiscal Year		Fiscal Year	
1954	transition year	1962	transition year
1955	83.12%	1963	95.52
1956	85.49	1964	86.34
1957	84.15	1965	83.81
1958	80.13	1966	85.90
1959	91.01	1967	82.00
1960	84.26	1968	82.17
1961	92.08	1969	82.30

objective of controlling defense expenditures by reducing the services' budget estimates after they were submitted in October.

A simple "random cut" model of budget reductions is suggested by a strategy which levies reductions without regard to the structure of the budget and differences among budget categories. This strategy would be equivalent to a decision to impose an *across-the-board percentage cut* on the services' budget estimates. In order to compare the predictions of this model with the observations from the Eisenhower administration, the amount requested by the services for each budget line item was calculated as a percentage of the total budget request. The budget reduction each line item suffered during the budget review was calculated as a percentage of the total budget reduction. A correlation coefficient was computed between the two resulting percentages across line items, by fiscal year.

This "across-the-board" strategy would be minimally supported if the correlations were positive and more strongly if the values of the correlations approached unity. As can be seen in table 15, however, the correlation coefficients are negative and of relatively small magnitudes. The data do not support the hypothesis that the Eisenhower administration imposed across-the-board percentage budget reductions.

Table 15. Correlation between Proportional Share of Budget and Proportional Share of Reduction, by Line Item

Fiscal Year	Correlation	Fiscal Year	Correlation
1954	transition year	1962	transition year
1955	—0.22	1963	—0.13
1956	—0.10	1964	—0.17
1957	—0.18	1965	—0.12
1958	—0.12	1966	—0.19
1959	—0.19	1967	—0.17
1960	—0.07	1968	—0.02
1961	—0.24	1969	—0.21

The sign of the correlations sheds light on another budget-cutting strategy. The administration might try to minimize its effort in the budget-cutting exercise by *concentrating reductions* in a few large— and therefore prominent—budget categories. If the civilian leadership did follow this rule, the slope of the regression line would exceed 1.00. The generally negative correlation coefficients demonstrate that this strategy was not invoked. On the contrary, there appears to have been a modest tendency to exact relatively larger reductions in some of the smaller line items.

The two preceding budget-cutting strategies have assumed that the civilian leadership took the initiative in allocating the reductions in the services' budgets. However, the McNamara description implies that the Eisenhower administration yielded substantial discretion to the services. This suggests a budget-cutting model in which the administration specified the total amount of the necessary reduction and left it to the services to allocate their shares of the reduction as they saw fit.

One such model simply would have the services assign themselves *equal shares of the reduction*, independent of their respective shares of the total budget estimate. However, as can be seen in table 16, each service's share of the reduction varied substantially during the Eisenhower administration, and in no year (with the possible exception of FY 1960) was the annual budget reduction allocated with rough equality among the three services. The rule that the services suffer equal shares of the budget cut was not followed during the Eisenhower years.

Alternatively, the services may have divided the reduction among themselves according to a "fair-share" decision rule. For example,

Table 16. Percentage Share of Budget Reduction, by Service

Fiscal Year	Army	Navy	Air Force
1954		transition year	
1955	32.01%	28.26%	39.74%
1956	24.51	34.31	41.18
1957	16.19	34.18	49.63
1958	33.29	15.56	51.15
1959	22.48	9.04	68.48
1960	36.89	34.13	28.98
1961	63.05	8.53	28.42
1962		transition year	
1963	49.06	13.99	36.95
1964	17.27	38.84	43.90
1965	18.51	34.87	46.62
1966	27.28	35.64	37.08
1967	28.41	29.11	42.49
1968	22.80	48.09	29.11
1969	27.19	36.98	35.83

each service might agree to absorb a share of the budget *reduction in proportion* to its share of the total three-service budget request. If the services had adhered to that guideline, their respective budget shares in the defense budget which Eisenhower sent to Congress would have been the same as their shares of the sum of the service submissions to the secretary.

To test this hypothesis, each service's percentage share of the total budget submitted by the services was calculated. Each services' percentage share of the reduction in the sum of their budget estimates also was computed. The absolute difference for these shares was summed across the three services. These sums should approach zero to the extent that the Eisenhower administration allowed the services to allocate the budget cut among themselves and they did so in proportion to their budget shares. As can be seen in table 17, however, in no year was the budget reduction apportioned according to each service's share of the budget. On the contrary, the sum of the absolute differences increased rather steadily throughout the Eisenhower years.

Table 17. Allocation of Budget Reduction, by Service

Fiscal Year	Sum of Absolute Differences	Fiscal Year	Sum of Absolute Differences
1954	transition year	1962	transition year
1955	9.09	1963	45.11
1956	10.40	1964	16.12
1957	11.73	1965	12.69
1958	22.41	1966	7.12
1959	38.12	1967	7.21
1960	31.07	1968	28.84
1961	72.09	1969	11.06

A different model of the allocation of the administration-imposed budget reduction yields opposite predictions. It might be argued that each service seeks to *minimize its share of the budget reduction* and that the "stronger" the service the more successful it is in achieving that objective. Using respective budget share as an index of relative strength, this model predicts that the larger a service's share of the sum of the services' budget estimates, the smaller its share of the budget reduction.

To evaluate this prediction, service budget shares were compared to the ratio of the proportional budget reduction to the budget share. The model predicts that the dominant service (as measured by the magnitude of the budget estimates) will suffer less than its share of the reduction (i.e., ratio less than 1.0) with the difference being made up by the weaker service(s). Specifically, the model predicts an inverse relation between the two variables.

When the cut ratio was regressed on the budget share for the Eisenhower years, no relationship was discernible: $r = 0.011$. Indeed, an inspection of the scatterplot revealed very wide dispersion and no identifiable relationships. That is, there was no regular association between a service's budget share and its relative proportion of the budget reduction during the Eisenhower administration.

The extent of service discretion in allocating resources within a fiscal constraint can be probed further by examining the distribution of the budget among appropriations categories. The officers and civilians who were interviewed agreed that, given the choice, the services will seek to preserve and expand the force structure at the expense of maintaining operational readiness.[7] This priority translates into the budgetary decision of concentrating the required reductions in Operation and Maintenance (O & M) in order to protect the Procurement budget. In addition, since appropriations for Procurement ordinarily are expended over several years, while O & M expenditures are concentrated in the first year, an administration seeking to maximize the near-term fiscal impact of any budget reductions would concentrate those cuts in the O & M account.[8]

Accordingly, if the portrayal of the Eisenhower administration as one primarily concerned with limiting spending and granting considerable discretion to the services is correct, there would have been mutually reinforcing incentives to concentrate budget reductions in the O & M account. To test this prediction, each budget category's relative share of the administration's reduction in the services' estimates was computed as the ratio of the proportion of the total budget cut taken in that account to the proportion of that category's percentage of the total defense budget. The results are shown in table 18.

These data also fail to support a description of the Eisenhower administration as one predominantly motivated by fiscal concerns. Without exception Procurement suffered more than its "fair share" of the total reduction. Except for FY 1956, Operation and Maintenance received less than its "fair share" of the reduction (in most years, considerably less). The results are precisely the opposite of those predicted: the military services were unable to "protect" their Procurement budget from disproportionate reductions, and the Ei-

Table 18. Ratio of Reduction Share to Budget Share, Procurement and Operation and Maintenance

Fiscal Year	Operation & Maintenance	Procurement	Fiscal Year	Operation & Maintenance	Procurement
1954	transition year		1962	transition year	
1955	0.99	1.65	1963	1.52	2.16
1956	1.35	1.52	1964	0.54	1.48
1957	0.49	1.95	1965	0.51	1.78
1958	0.42	1.81	1966	0.41	2.04
1959	0.64	2.03	1967	0.64	1.76
1960	0.31	1.77	1968	0.73	1.76
1961	0.37	1.76	1969	0.01	1.86

senhower administration exacted its cuts in that part of the budget in which the fiscal consequences were attenuated.

A more detailed analysis of the procurement budget indicates that the services also were unable to protect the *specific* procurement categories which they considered to be most vital. There is a separate budget line item which aggregates the costs of procuring aircraft for the Air Force. Since the Air Force defines its raison d'être as the flying of aircraft, this item's share of the annual budget reduction should illuminate the Air Force's ability to protect those areas which it considers important.[9] Similarly, naval aviation was the dominant branch in the Navy during the 1950s, and the budget for the Navy's aircraft and missiles also is segregated in a separate line item.[10]

A test of each service's latitude of discretion would be its success in protecting that part of the budget reflected in these line items. Each line item's share of the annual budget reduction was computed as the ratio of the line item's share of the budget reduction to its share of the budget request. The annual ratios of reduction to budget shares for Air Force aircraft procurement and Navy aircraft and missile procurement are shown in table 19.

The data reveal that these services were unable to protect even their most vital functions from disproportionately large budget reductions during the Eisenhower administration. In the majority of cases both the Air Force and Navy suffered large budget reductions in these areas and, frequently, very large cuts. In only one case—Navy aircraft and missile procurement in FY 1961—were these budget accounts treated with special favor. In three other cases, the

Table 19. Ratio of Reduction Share to Budget Share, Aircraft Procurement

Fiscal Year	Navy Aircraft and Missiles	Air Force Aircraft	Fiscal Year	Navy Aircraft and Missiles	Air Force Aircraft
1954	transition year		1962	transition year	
1955	1.25	1.20	1963	0.19	3.67
1956	2.66	1.04	1964	2.16	0.75
1957	2.14	1.59	1965	1.87	1.64
1958	0.92	1.76	1966	1.98	1.12
1959	2.38	2.27	1967	2.31	1.93
1960	1.71	0.96	1968	2.67	1.28
1961	0.63	3.71	1969	1.90	1.95

reductions were in rough proportion to the line item's share of the total budget request. In the remaining ten cases, the line items' share of the budget reduction exceeded their proportion of the budget request by a considerable margin. In sum, if we conservatively assume that, given the choice, the Air Force and the Navy would not take greater than "fair share" cuts in their aircraft budgets, then we may conclude that Eisenhower did not leave the choice to them.

Our examination of the defense budget during the 1950s has painted a somewhat different picture of the Eisenhower administration than that which was offered by its successor as the rationale for PPBS. Whatever the explanation for the Eisenhower administration's defense budget decisions, it must go beyond a simple model of crude fiscal control innocent of any defense policy preferences.

Budget-Making as Policy-Making in the Eisenhower Administration
The analysis of the procurement budget during the 1950s suggests an alternative explanation for the motives and behavior of the Eisenhower administration. If an administration were seeking to shape and direct defense programs by means of the budget, the most potent leverage points relate to the funding of weapons systems, that is, to the procurement accounts. As Hitch observed (1965, p. 23): "These [weapons systems] choices . . . have become . . . the key decisions around which much else of the defense program revolves." That is, the results shown in tables 18 and 19 are consistent with a description of an Eisenhower administration which exercised its national security *policy* preferences through the operations of the defense *budget* cycle.[11]

It would have been extraordinary for Eisenhower, the career soldier and five-star general, to have been indifferent about defense policies and programs. As he observed in his memoirs (1963, p. 445): "my military background assured at least that as President I would hold certain definite convictions on national security." For example, he reduced the service budget estimates for FY 1954 (prepared under Truman) by about $5 billion, an amount which came almost entirely from the Air Force budget. Truman's goal of 143 air wings by 1955 was reduced by the Eisenhower administration to 120 wings. These changes, Eisenhower wrote to a congressman, represented his "own views" and had his "personal endorsement" (quoted in Congressional Quarterly 1953, pp. 137–38).[12]

More important, the record indicates that Eisenhower recognized the linkage between defense policy and the budget and that he operated on the latter to affect the former. Ironically, much of the 1950s' criticism of defense management focused on the administration's exploitation of the budget process to influence defense policy. Where the 1948 Hoover Commission recommended that the secretary of defense have full power over the budget, the 1955 Hoover Commission was distressed that the OSD Comptroller "has had to deal with *matters of operating policy* beyond the usual responsibility of comptrollership" (quoted in Hammond 1961, p. 305, emphasis added). Subsequent congressional hearings highlighted the continuing policy influence of the comptroller. Hammond reports (1961, p. 306): "In 1958 Congressional investigations of military research and development produced a wide variety of evidence that the Comptroller continued to exercise considerable control over the services beyond what was regarded as a comptrolling function."

Maxwell Taylor, one of the Eisenhower administration's harshest critics, also acknowledged the policy impact of Eisenhower's budget-making. For example, when he was asked by the Jackson Subcommittee whether Eisenhower had personally considered "the pace at which we ought to modernize the Army's weapons," Taylor replied (U.S. Congress, Senate, 1961, Part I, pp. 795–96):

> I am sure he did in recent years *because the issue was laid out very clearly in our budgetary discussion. . . .* It always got to the President at the time of the presentation of the budget where the services were able to comment on the effect of the budget on their own service. [Emphasis added][3]

These comments—and complaints—of his contemporaries suggest that for Eisenhower, as for McNamara, the budget was the blueprint of the administration's defense policy, and the budget process was the mechanism for monitoring compliance. As Mc-

Namara was to do in a more elaborate and systematic fashion, Eisenhower exploited his bargaining resources to dominate the internal allocation of the defense budget in order to achieve his objectives and to promote compliance. (And, as will be seen in Chapter 7, both administrations used the resource allocation process to manipulate the services' incentives.) As Wilfred McNeil, Pentagon comptroller from 1949 to 1959, remarked: "In reading some of the material presenting the [McNamara defense management] plan . . . , I would be forced to conclude that there is some lack of knowledge of what has been the general practice for some years" (U.S. Congress, Senate, 1961, Part I, p. 1060).

Budget-Making and Policy-Making in the 1960s

Perhaps more striking than the poor fit between 1950s budget data and predictions of budget-cutting models, is the considerable similarity between the results for the 1950s and for the 1960s. As shown in tables 14 through 19, the data fit about as well (or as poorly) for the Eisenhower administration as for the Kennedy-Johnson period. The absence of any substantial differences between the two time periods is particularly noteworthy since the analysis has concentrated on that part of the annual budget cycle—the October to January budget review—in which the contrasts between the Republicans and Democrats should have been greatest. However, the services' budget estimates were reduced by roughly the same amount during McNamara's tenure as during the Eisenhower years. In neither time period was the review of the services' estimates a routine bookkeeping exercise. During *all* of the years under review, the services' budgets underwent major surgery before being presented to Congress.[14]

Part of the explanation for these similarities already has been suggested: whatever the objectives of the Eisenhower administration's budget rules, they were not simply and completely to balance the budget. On the contrary, the analysis indicates that the Eisenhower administration achieved many of the objectives claimed for the McNamara budget system, although less formally and perhaps less comprehensively.

Analysis of the McNamara system offers a convergent explanation which is the obverse of the account of the Eisenhower period. In particular, the monitoring capabilities of PPBS were less than anticipated (or assumed), and, more important, fiscal concerns, although not openly acknowledged, imposed a significant constraint on the operation of the McNamara budget system and on the choices which emerged.

Upgrading Monitoring Capabilities: The Five-Year Defense Program

Mechanisms and procedures which monitor the behavior of subordinates—provide "administrative feedback" in Kaufman's phrase (1973)—affect the probability that subordinate noncompliance will be detected and, accordingly, its frequency and extent. To the extent that the noncompliance which is uncovered is inadvertent, little more than detection is required for its amelioration. We also would expect the probability of deliberate noncompliance to be inversely related to the probability of detection, even if detection were not reliably accompanied by negative sanctions: internalized norms and pressures from peers make it difficult to sustain actions which are regarded by others, as well as by oneself, as illegitimate (Simon, Smithburg, and Thompson 1970).

The official view of the Kennedy administration (U.S. Department of Defense, *Milestones*) was that the inadequacies of Eisenhower's mechanisms for monitoring the services' compliance "may have been the most critical weakness of the pre-PPBS operation." The device of the Five-Year Defense Program (FYDP) promised to monitor—and thus improve—military compliance in the context of the budget process.

The FYDP was the compilation of defense programs which had been approved by the secretary of defense, costed-out for five years. According to Enthoven and Smith (1971, p. 49):

> [The FYDP] . . . is an authoritative record of what the Secretary of Defense has tentatively approved for purposes of force and financial planning. In other words, all interested parties within DOD know how many and what kinds of divisions, squadrons, ships, etc. have been authorized and how many men and how much money it will take to support them.

In principle, the services could request funds in their annual budget estimates only for those programs as approved in the FYDP. The FYDP could be amended only with the explicit approval of the secretary. In the view of William Kaufmann (1964, pp. 202–3):

> He [McNamara] had sponsored the planning-programming-budgeting process in such a way that the Secretary could now exercise

an unprecedented degree of real control over the formulation and execution of defense policy.

Thus the FYDP should have been a mechanism ideally suited to an administration committed to actively designing and directing its own national security program at the expense of severely reducing the services' scope of discretion.

However, there was nothing formally logical (as contrasted with reasonable) about the program structure: the FYDP lacked mutually exclusive and exhaustive categories. Instead, the division of the total force structure into programs was based on notions of what were the most important issues and useful comparisons, and which components could be assumed to be substantially independent of one another. Accordingly, the program elements included within the various programs were spread across a range of categories and levels of aggregation. Forces identified as individual program elements included battalions and divisions; categories which composed the program elements included individual weapons under development, aircraft squadrons, and Army divisions. Although several program elements were weapons systems, not every weapons system was identified as a program element. As judgments based on these criteria changed, so did the structure of the FYDP. As a consequence, the Five-Year Defense Program was both complex and incomplete.

Since not every object of expenditure—which ultimately had to be included in the annual budget—appeared in the FYDP, "planning factors" which approximated these costs frequently were substituted. The annual budget estimates necessarily replaced these planning factors with projected expenditures for the next fiscal year. An internal Defense Department analysis describes the problem:

> The FYDP may include a *factor* of $50,000 per aircraft per year for depot-level maintenance of a particular aircraft, or $800,000 if 16 such aircraft are in the program. The budget will reflect the overhauls *actually scheduled* for 1969, considering time between overhauls and recent cost experience. The budget amount may be zero, $2 million, $800,000, or some other number. Many items of great significance . . . are not specified in the force and manpower tables of the FYDP, nor well reflected in the factors. [Emphasis added]

A significant proportion of each annual budget—estimated by one former DOD official at from 25 to 40 percent—did not appear in the FYDP in a budgetable form. As a result, the October to January budget review remained a "crunch" during the 1960s in large measure because the annual budget estimates could *not* be derived directly from the FYDP.

A related problem concerned the allocation of fixed costs. A portion of the defense budget represents "operating expenses" which would be incurred regardless of the presence or absence of any particular program. However, these costs somehow must be assigned to the various program elements included in the FYDP if that document is to reflect the annual cost of the overall defense program. As Charles Hitch acknowledged (1965, p. 65):

> Many of the alleged "actual" operating costs in the Five-Year program are obtained by an *arbitrary* allocation of budget categories. . . . For example, *we do not really know* whether the Army's present cost projections accurately reflect the growing operation and maintenance requirements of its expanding fleet of aircraft.[15] [Emphasis added]

Even when costs could be directly related to a particular activity, there frequently remained some ambiguity regarding the specific FYDP program (or program element) to which those costs should be allocated. In the absence of an explicit directive addressing each ambiguity on a case-by-case basis, the decision unavoidably was left to the subordinate's discretion.

These defects in the FYDP had important consequences for the conflicts between the civilians and the military. The gulf between the FYDP and the budget estimates meant that the annual battle between the services and the secretary did not end when the programming phase of the budget cycle was concluded. Contrary to expectations—and to popular descriptions of PPBS in the Defense Department—program decisions did *not* imply budgetary decisions. A senior civilian Army official complained to the incoming Nixon administration in an internal memorandum:

> When operations commenced under the new OSD program system in 1962, it was the general understanding that program decisions would be budget decisions. This euphoric supposition lasted only until the fall of the same year when it became apparent . . . that program decisions were not, literally, budget decisions. This situation has prevailed over the years. . . . OSD approval of the FYDP . . . does not constitute a budgetary decision.

But if secretarial approval of a program did not entail budgetary support for it, neither did the absence of an approved program in the FYDP necessarily prohibit a service from seeking funds for a new or expanded function in its budget estimates. On the contrary, the services continued to press for their policy preferences and organizational objectives as they prepared their budget estimates. One colonel reported that during the latter part of the Johnson administration the number of formal Army requests for changes in the FYDP decreased sharply. He attributed the decline in large measure to the fact that they were unnecessary: there was sufficient ambiguity in the FYDP for the Army to budget funds for new or expanded programs without going to the secretary for formal program approval.[16]

In principle, the FYDP was a mechanism which minimized subordinate discretion and constrained noncompliance. In practice, it was a mechanism with important gaps and overlaps, as well as considerable ambiguity and arbitrariness. The incomplete structure of the FYDP necessarily delegated some of the responsibility for its operation to the services while its complexity tended to obscure instances in which the services did not distribute costs according to the civilians' intentions. In many ways, the FYDP, one of whose objectives was to increase OSD's capacity to monitor the services, itself imposed an enormous monitoring burden on the civilians. Instead of checking for substantive compliance with the administration's defense programs, the civilians found themselves checking for procedural compliance with the rules of the FYDP.[17]

McNamara as a Budget Cutter

The ambiguous relationship between program decisions and budget decisions was symptomatic of the omnipresent, but unacknowledged, fiscal constraint which colored the operations of PPBS. The manner in which the Eisenhower administration decided how much was enough for defense became an important issue in the 1960 presidential campaign. Candidate Kennedy charged the Republicans with endangering the country's security by imposing an "arbitrary" (and presumably inadequate) ceiling on defense spending.

The shift away from the Eisenhower administration's emphasis on fiscal objectives continued to be the difference most emphasized by the spokesmen for PPBS. McNamara told reporters in 1964 (quoted in Harrelson 1968, p. 226): "I want to emphasize, we don't build the defense program against a pre-determined budget limit and I don't make any effort to add up the proposals of the Services."[18] McNamara frequently reiterated this "no ceilings" principle, not only in the public record but also in internal documents. For example, in a then-*classified* memorandum to Lyndon Johnson reporting on the FY 1966 defense budget, McNamara wrote (Mc-

Namara, 1964): "The recommended force structure [to be funded by the proposed FY 1966 budget] was based on requirements for national security and was not limited by arbitrary or predetermined budget ceilings." This assurance apparently was routinely included in McNamara's annual classified memoranda to Kennedy and Johnson concerning the forthcoming defense budget.

However, there is considerable evidence which suggests that there *was* a ceiling on the defense budget in approximately the same sense —and with many of the same consequences—as existed during the Eisenhower administration. For example, as shown in table 14, Mc-Namara regularly reduced the budget estimates submitted by the military services: the services always asked for "too much" for approved programs as measured by some standard. As one Air Force officer observed sardonically: "McNamara always insisted there was no budget ceiling but regularly made all kinds of cuts to get under it." Likewise, the U.S. Blue Ribbon Defense Panel (1970) noted that the annual defense total implied in the FYDP always exceeded the size of the president's defense budget request to Congress.

Crecine (1969) has demonstrated that the overall federal budgetary process operated in such a manner during the Kennedy-Johnson years that the total amount available for defense spending (within a narrow limit) *must* have been known prior to the time that the services were required to submit their budget estimates to the secretary. Hitch acknowledged this early in the Kennedy administration (U.S. Congress, Senate, 1961, Part I, p. 1033):

> Certainly at some point the Secretary of Defense and the President and the Director of the Bureau of the Budget have to decide what the limit is for the Department of Defense as a whole. . . . You can begin with some idea about the likely limit for the Defense Department as a whole in *June*. . . . [Emphasis added]

There was then, according to common usage, an annual "ceiling" on defense spending during McNamara's tenure.

More important, the evidence suggests that the timing of McNamara's decisions on *program changes* in the FYDP reflected his need to reconcile the costs of approved programs with a predetermined ceiling. Since the budgeting phase of PPBS was intended to be a routine costing out of approved programs, the debate over changes in the FYDP should have been substantially completed prior to early October, when the services submitted their budget estimates. The system, however, did not operate according to these expectations. The programming phase regularly ran into, and overlapped with, the budget review (Hitch 1965, p. 64).[19]

This overlap was due in part to the services' procrastination and maneuvering. An internal Defense Department memorandum observed: "The Military Departments have typically delayed submission of large numbers of PCRs [requests for FYDP changes] until late in the calendar year program budget cycles" (quoted in Crecine 1969). However, OSD made its own contribution to the persistent overlap between the programming and budgeting phases. One Army official complained in an internal Pentagon memorandum:

> OSD for its part has been capricious in its consideration of PCRs —early submission has not correlated with early action in the form of Program Change Decisions (PCDs). The result has been that half or more of all PCRs have been "folded" by OSD into the budget review process.

That is, even when the services sought secretarial approval for changes in the FYDP prior to the preparation of their budget estimates, OSD postponed its decisions on defense programs until the October deadline for the submission of budget estimates had passed.

Not only did this contribute to the problems of generating budget estimates from the FYDP, but it cast serious doubts on the credibility of the formal PPBS procedures. This behavior created incentives for the services to postpone submission of PCRs; it also strongly suggested that there was a known—if unannounced—annual spending limit for defense. Indeed, in a 1962 letter to Hitch, the Army argued that the pattern of civilian review of the services' PCRs strongly suggested that there *was* a defense budget ceiling. It called for making these resource constraints explicit so that the services' program change proposals could take account of them (U.S. Bureau of the Budget 1962).

As the Army implied, the timing of OSD's responses to PCRs is consistent with the hypothesis that the number of program changes which could be approved was constrained by an implicit ceiling on the defense budget. As one OSD official acknowledged:

> Ninety percent of the (program) decision documents were written after December 28 [i.e., about two and a half months after the services had submitted their *budget* estimates]. The reason for this "piling" of key decisions toward the end of the budget cycle is because the Secretary of Defense cannot afford to commit himself early on major decisions and still maintain any flexibility. He has to see how the wind is blowing on the federal budget, particularly in regard to the total. He has to see what the price tag on the hard core of the defense budget looks like.[20] [Quoted in Crecine 1969, p. 37]

A meeting between Bureau of the Budget and Pentagon representatives on the FY 1967 budget provides a good illustration of the intrinsic problem with McNamara's budgeting system. BOB raised the question of how many nuclear attack submarines should be procured in the coming year. As an internal memorandum on that meeting makes clear (U.S., Department of Defense, Office of the Secretary of Defense 1965), a decision about submarines had to await better information about the magnitude of defense budget total. The BOB and Pentagon officials agreed in that meeting that: "This issue is to be held in abeyance *until the overall FY 1967 budget situation has been determined*" (emphasis added).

In brief, McNamara's program decisions had to be postponed until his review of the services' budget estimates was completed. Contrary to popularized descriptions of defense budget-making during the 1960s, the annual defense budget was not calculated simply by adding up the costs of the activities required for national security. McNamara did not have a blank check, and he worked hard, if not openly, to keep his spending within predetermined limits.

Conclusion

The rhetoric of defense decision-makers in the 1960s implied dramatic contrasts between their predecessors and themselves in the use of the budgeting process as a policy instrument. However, our analysis of budget data from the two time periods reveals striking similarities, if not essentially indistinguishable behavior. The record suggests that the political leadership of the Eisenhower administration appreciated and exploited the opportunities for control of national security policy that are inherent in the defense budgeting mechanism. The political leadership of the Kennedy and Johnson administrations was hounded by, and yielded to, the same fiscal pressures that played so prominent a role in the popular image of the Eisenhower years. As a result, the civilians in the Kennedy-Johnson administration "found themselves in a position with respect to the services that was not as different from that of their predecessors as they might have wished" (Stromberg 1970, p. 124).

More important than the Democrats' ungenerous portrayal of defense budgeting during the 1950s was their own inability to overcome persistent obstacles to the implementation of their policy preferences. Their behavior and choices were limited by many of the same constraints that operated during the Eisenhower administration. Neither public disclaimers of unavoidable resource limitations nor new management techniques which remained insensitive to organizational dilemmas and participants' incentives produced the consequences sought by their proponents. Whatever the differences between the 1950s and the 1960s, the intended consequences of the formal PPBS system bear little of the responsibility.

However, there *was* a McNamara Revolution in the Pentagon in the 1960s. Interactions among the participants were different. Many of these changes can be traced back to the operation of PPBS, if not to the theory. Moreover, several of these changes appear to have been unexpected and, from the perspective of the civilians, undesirable. These unintended consequences of formal reorganization are the subject of the next chapter.

6

Budget-making as Policy-making
The Unintended Consequences

If PPBS was the instrument of the McNamara Revolution, its agent was the Office of the Secretary of Defense (OSD). As measured both by budgets and personnel, OSD experienced marked growth during the 1960s.

The expansion of the OSD budget is one indication of McNamara's efforts to assert his leadership and control. OSD's share of the annual budget request to Congress is shown in table 20. Although OSD's budget began to grow relative to those of the services during the second Eisenhower administration, it experienced sharp and steady increases during the 1960s.[1] Approximately 3 percent of the last defense budget Eisenhower submitted to Congress was allocated to OSD. Five years later its share had increased to 7.7 percent. Prior to Vietnam, the yearly increase in the OSD budget during the 1960s ranged from 30 to 90 percent of the annual budget increment. During the Eisenhower administration, by contrast, OSD's budget fared much less well: in two years the budget included fewer funds for OSD than had been appropriated the preceding year, and OSD never absorbed more than 13 percent of the annual increment.

The increasing numbers of civilian personnel employed by the Office of the Secretary of Defense support the picture painted by the budget data. OSD contracted in size during most of the Eisenhower administration. McNamara's tenure, by contrast, witnessed a steady increase in the number of OSD civilian personnel. The number of civilians grew by more than 50 percent between FY 1962 and FY 1969. In FY 1958 there were 3.7 civilians in OSD per 1,000 commissioned officers; by FY 1967, there were nearly 6 civilians in OSD per 1,000 commissioned officers.[2]

Although this pattern of growth is consistent with an image of aggressive leadership at the secretarial level, the absolute size of the office highlights its persisting vulnerability to overload. Relative to the size of the defense bureaucracy, OSD remained very small. Severe limits on the Office's capabilities to enforce the secretary's decisions and to detect noncompliance persisted throughout McNamara's tenure. When peak employment was reached in FY 1968, there were still fewer than 2,300 civilians employed by the Office of the Secretary of Defense. Moreover, more than 60 percent of these personnel were secretarial and junior professional staff, that is, below the grade of GS-11. To the extent that McNamara's innovations presumed extensive monitoring and detailed enforcement, their prospects for success depended on a very modest organizational capability. These circumstances would seem to suggest that a secretary of defense should husband his bargaining resources and be sensitive to the incentives which confront the participants whom he is trying to influence.

Table 20. OSD Budget as a Percentage of Total Defense Budget Request

Fiscal Year	OSD as % of total defense budget	Fiscal Year	OSD as % of total defense budget
(1954[a]	2.66)	(1962[a]	3.25)
1955	1.82	1963	4.29
1956	2.08	1964	6.06
1957	1.87	1965	7.05
1958	1.83	1966	7.73
1959	3.09	1967	6.50
1960	3.33	1968	6.67
1961	3.01	1969	6.25

[a]Presidential transition years.

Notwithstanding these limitations, the chroniclers of McNamara's tenure as secretary of defense suggest that he adopted a novel definition of that position: the hallmark of the McNamara Revolution was a conception of the secretary of defense as the initiator and architect of defense policy. Our budget analysis, however, does not reveal large differences between the Eisenhower and Kennedy-Johnson administrations in terms of their ability and willingness to enforce their policy preferences and choices. That analysis suggested that the Eisenhower administration, like its successors, used the budget—with mixed results—as an instrument of policy.

These results leave us with something of a puzzle: although the growth of OSD during the 1960s suggests the intention and the attempt, the data analysis casts doubt on McNamara's *success* in playing his self-proclaimed role as a stronger and more aggressive secretary of defense. Consideration of some of the unintended consequences of changes in budget-making—for the participants' bargaining resources and for the relations among them—will help to solve this puzzle.

Wielding Bargaining Advantages: The Bureaucratic Consequences of Strategic Doctrine

As we have seen, the president cannot routinely command obedience from the members of the national security bureaucracy. Rather, he must bargain for it. Nor does he monopolize the bargaining advantages by virtue of his claims to formal authority. On the contrary, his bargaining advantages, while powerful, are finite. Even if the president could successfully invoke his formal authority on any question, he cannot personally decide *every* question. He cannot personally monitor the behavior of all of his subordinates any more than he can intervene every time that an instance of noncompliance is discovered.

He can, however, create presumptions (cf. Arkes 1972) and distribute burdens of proof by announcing his substantive policy preferences and promulgating implementing directives. These changes in the "rules of the game" permit the president's bureaucratic supporters to invoke his formal authority. To the extent that his authoritative statements are successful in distributing burdens of proof, the president can strengthen his allies' bargaining advantages and reduce the frequency of challenges to his authority (Ponturo 1969).[3]

However, authoritative pronouncements vary in the effectiveness with which they exploit bargaining advantages deriving from formal authority. The efficacy of policy statements in curbing noncompliance depends upon their ability to create presumptions which bias outcomes in preferred directions, and on their capacity to distinguish actions which are congruent with the president's wishes from behavior which is incompatible.

However one judges the defense policies of the Eisenhower administration on strategic grounds, they did serve to reduce the burdens of detecting, identifying, and rejecting incompatible proposals and decisions. Once the doctrine of massive retaliation had been formalized (through the National Security Council machinery), it provided an authoritative standard against which to judge programs for compliance with the president's wishes. The doctrine was reinforced by Eisenhower's decision that, for planning purposes, the military services could assume that nuclear weapons would be used whenever they were judged militarily useful.

The effect of these presidential directives was to deny legitimacy to force and budget requirements based on plans for a large-scale or long-term nonnuclear conflict (Snyder 1962, p. 437). Moreover, the directives provided bargaining advantages to Eisenhower's allies as they sought to implement his decisions. Glenn Snyder has concluded (1962, pp. 439–40):

> Perhaps the most important effect of the decision was to provide Secretary Wilson and Admiral Radford with a formal justification for reducing these [Army and Navy] forces. The President . . . had now put his name to a policy obviously intended to stress air power and to justify Army and Navy cutbacks.

Another prominent feature of Eisenhower's defense policy was the replacement of the Truman administration's concept of the "year of critical danger" by the notion of preparing for the "long haul" as a basis for determining the size of military forces and budgets. The logic of the "long haul" meant that decisions regarding forces and budgets were substantially insulated from changes in the level of international tensions or Soviet military capabilities. Eisenhower insisted that the American defense effort could not be allowed to fluctuate "depending upon the state of world affairs" (quoted in Huntington 1961a, p. 68). As a consequence of this policy, a traditional source of justifications for increases in forces and budgets was denied to the military services and bargaining advantages were redistributed in favor of the civilian leadership.

Thus, Eisenhower acted in an area in which the authority of the civilians, particularly the president, was beyond challenge: designing national security policy and setting the outlines of military strategy. Eisenhower's strategic doctrine redistributed bargaining advantages by clearly distinguishing between those defense programs which served his ends and those which did not. Claims for increases in conventional forces did not have to be rejected on an individual basis; their proponents bore the heavy burden of being required to attack the foundations of the authoritative strategic doctrine.

The incoming Kennedy administration substituted the doctrine of "flexible response" for that of massive retaliation. This new strategic doctrine was based upon what William Kaufmann (1964) has called "the search for options." There was, reported McNamara, a conscious effort "to expand the range of military alternatives available to the President" (quoted in Kaufmann 1964, p. 67).

Whatever its merits as a strategic doctrine, flexible response did little to distribute burdens of proof in the decision-making process: it could not be convincingly invoked to block consideration of any defense program on its face.[4] All of the military services could, and did, claim that their highest-priority programs contributed options and flexibility to the country's military posture. The president's agents were compelled to confront and refute these challenges on a case-by-case basis, each time increasing the mutual irritation, weariness, and bitterness.

The case of the manned bomber is instructive. Although it was clear that the Kennedy administration was opposed to a follow-on manned bomber, the Air Force continued to argue for the project precisely on the grounds that it was the best way to add flexibility to our nuclear response (Roherty 1970, pp. 103–40). In refuting the Air Force's claims, McNamara was forced to resort to elaborate and subtle interpretations of what was and was not compatible with the administration's security objectives. The doctrine of flexible response did not settle the matter for him in any lasting way nor could he rely on the presumption of compliance to reduce his involvement.

The administration hoped that its official criteria for sizing strategic forces would supplement its strategic doctrine in resisting demands for more bombers and missiles. Henry Rowen (1975, p. 227) reports that McNamara saw in the doctrine of "assured destruction" "a basis for denying service and Congressional claims for more money for strategic forces." In time, however, McNamara discovered that the doctrine actually had created "pressures for additional forces and budgets" (Rowen 1975, p. 233). Unlike Eisenhower's concept of the long haul, the standards of "assured destruction" and "damage limitation" were explicitly linked to Soviet capabilities. Changes in these capabilities, and bureaucratic conflicts over estimates of those capabilities, provided recurring opportunities to reopen debates regarding the appropriate size of U.S. forces and the defense budget. As the decade progressed, the administration found itself modifying its strategic doctrine and abandoning core concepts (e.g., "no cities," "damage limitation") in order to constrain the bureaucratic pressures for expansion of military capabilities and expenditures.

Although the doctrine of flexible response failed to insulate the administration from constant claims and appeals as successfully as the doctrine of massive retaliation did, it might be thought that the FYDP—as a list of formally approved programs—would function as a superior alternative. As we have seen, however, the services increasingly came to feel that the FYDP imposed only modest constraints on their choice of programs and activities. The structure and content of the FYDP did little to establish general rules which impeded proposals in conflict with the administration's strategic preferences. On the contrary, the administration continually insisted, both by word and elaborate "updating" procedures, that no decision recorded in the FYDP was final.

Moreover, the sequence of decision-making under PPBS literally multiplied the opportunities to raise the same dispute for authoritative resolution in each annual budget cycle: once as part of the exchange of Draft Presidential Memoranda during the planning phase; a second time as the FYDP was "updated" during the programming phase; and a third time in the services' annual budget estimates.

Far from substituting for the functions performed by strategic doctrine during the Eisenhower administration, McNamara's budgeting system tended to expand the range of decisions which the civilians had to confront and to multiply the number of times each issue had to be faced. PPBS did little to establish authoritative presumptions which the services would have to surmount. Changes in the formal rules which accompanied the McNamara Revolution did not protect the administration's bargaining advantages from depletion.

Wielding Bargaining Advantages: Responses to the Challenge of Functional Authority

The president also must confront and subdue implicit challenges to his authority from his subordinates. Peabody (1962, p. 465) distinguishes between "formal authority" and "functional authority." The president has overwhelming formal authority, that is, formal powers which attach to whomever occupies that office. Functional authority derives from the possession of a scarce and valuable skill, what Victor Thompson (1961) describes as "personal specialization." The functional authority of the president's uniformed subordinates derives from their claim to unique possession of the needed expertise. When the loci of functional authority and formal authority do not coincide, the former may serve as a basis for challenge to the latter (Peabody 1962, pp. 466, 470).

It is virtually impossible to find any senior American officer who will question the formal authority of politically accountable decision-makers. The doctrine of civilian control of the military is deeply internalized as well as publicly proclaimed. However unwise they may believe the strategic doctrine and policy guidance to be, however inadequate they may think their resources are, professional military officers acknowledge the authority of the president to set the outlines of national security policy and to adjudicate among the competing claims on the federal budget.

In certain limited areas, the civilians reciprocate by acknowledging the military's implicit claims of functional authority. The conduct of military operations is one such area, and the development and prosecution of the "search and destroy" operations during the Vietnam War provide a good illustration.[5] Initially a supporter, McNamara became increasingly skeptical of General Westmoreland's strategy for the ground war in the south. He did little, however, to change that strategy. As he explained in a 1967 interview, he did not interfere with Westmoreland's programs because he lacked the requisite military experience; he was obliged to defer to his professional military officers who, in turn, respected the autonomy of the field commander (Gallucci 1975, pp. 389, 392).

The respective realms of the civilians and the military, however, necessarily are ill-defined and inevitably overlap. Civilian claims of functional authority frequently provoke military skepticism, if not hostility.[6] Moreover, military officers may doubt the civilians' competence to make "military" decisions and to choose among "military" alternatives. These reservations mitigate the imperatives of compliance (Peabody 1962, p. 466n). As a result, the president's preponderance of formal authority does not reliably protect him from challenges to his defense programs that derive from appeals to the military's functional authority.

The services' invocation of functional authority, however, represents an opportunity as well as a threat. As Chapter 4 suggested, the president views the military's claim of expertise with some ambivalence: while he must avoid becoming hostage to the services' priorities, he would prefer to invoke their functional authority in support of his national security programs. This dilemma can be ameliorated by two maneuvers. First, the administration can attempt to introduce criteria for choosing among defense alternatives which are beyond the boundaries of claimed expertise, that is, to insist that military expertise is a necessary—but not the sole—element in the formulation of national security policy. Second, the claims of unique expertise and appeals to functional authority can be impugned.

The Eisenhower administration and the successor Democratic administrations used both maneuvers. The relative emphasis placed on each technique by the different administrations, however, runs contrary to expectations. The administration headed by a former five-star general and war hero—who could persuasively claim personal possession of the necessary expertise—tended to avoid direct challenges to the military's functional authority. Instead, it emphasized criteria for choice which were beyond the professional competence of the officers. During McNamara's tenure, by contrast, the administration frequently appeared to claim a special competence in areas which previously had been the exclusive preserve of the services. At the same time, it rarely voiced—and frequently excluded—nonmilitary choice criteria.

Eisenhower only rarely invoked the argument that, by virtue of his training and experience, he was professionally competent to decide issues requiring military expertise.[7] Instead, and in a departure from the practice of the Truman administration, the Joint Chiefs of Staff were instructed that the strength of the domestic economy made a direct contribution to the national security. Consequently, the Chiefs were obliged to consider the economic consequences of their proposals and to constrain their recommendations by reference to budgetary feasibility (Snyder 1962, pp. 430–31). This explicit consideration of economic factors in JCS deliberations had the dual objective of limiting the Chiefs' recommendations while securing their support.[8]

The introduction of the economic consequences of military proposals also served another function. The inclusion of criteria which were beyond the professional competence of the Chiefs permitted the services' recommendations to be rejected on other than military grounds: their requests could be denied without challenging the foundations of military professionalism. Thus, the Eisenhower administration could "agree in principle" with a service's estimate of the contribution a proposal would make to the national defense but could postpone or avoid implementation by reference to the projected fiscal consequences.

President Kennedy also instructed the Joint Chiefs to go beyond narrow military factors in framing their advice and to consider political, economic, and social factors as well (Sorensen 1966, p. 605). However, the Joint Chiefs were not obliged to constrain their recommendations out of a concern for budgetary feasibility (Harrelson 1968). On the contrary, the administration insisted that the economy could tolerate whatever expenditures were required.

An economic calculus continued to play a central role in the civilians' response to military recommendations. However, the emphasis shifted from a concern with macroeconomic consequences to a concern for the efficient allocation of resources. This change in emphasis was accompanied by a shift in the civilians' response to the military's assertion of functional authority.

"Systems analysis" was portrayed as an analytical technique which would assist in choosing among alternatives in terms of the new economic criterion. It also was the Democratic administration's primary response to the services' claim of unique expertise. Having no one with the military credentials of an Eisenhower, the Kennedy administration could resort to systems analysis as a way to legitimate military decisions which were not endorsed by the military services. As Legere and Davis have observed (1969a, p. 177): "McNamara was a blessing to Kennedy because the new President needed the kind of detailed, systematic evidence that McNamara's procedures provided before he ran the risk of overruling the professional military."

The introduction of systems analysis into defense decision-making is an example of the redistribution of bargaining advantages among the participants through a change in the formal rules. McNamara's insistence—based upon his formal authority—that alternatives be derived from a particular analytical approach permitted him to structure the definition of the problem and to stipulate the criteria for choice (Hammond 1968, p. 63). However, the adoption of systems analysis also struck at the heart of the military's presumption of expertise. The services responded with bitterness and obstruction.

Previously there had been a conflict-muting division of labor. Politically responsible civilian officials established the nation's security objectives and consulted with their senior military advisors regarding potential threats to those objectives. The military exercised their special competence to select the most appropriate means to counter the threats identified and to achieve the chosen objectives—within whatever constraints the administration might impose.

The implications of systems analysis entailed a two-pronged assault which denied this division of labor and which challenged the foundations of military professionalism. First, OSD required the services to *defend* their recommendations and proposals: the civilians no longer would accept the professional judgments of the officers. In the words of Paul Hammond (1968, p. 63), the system administered by McNamara denied "to certain professional military groups the privilege of deciding without explaining."

Second, OSD asserted its competence, not merely to evaluate the services' analyses, but also to reject them and to substitute the recommendations made by the young civilians with no military training and experience who staffed the Office of Systems Analysis. Indeed, until the services became adequately proficient in the jargon and the techniques, McNamara was able to exploit their inability to respond with satisfactory analyses as a basis for rejecting their proposals. Thus, when he rejected a unanimous JCS recommendation that the program to develop an improved surface-to-air missile for bomber defense be accelerated, it was with the explanation that "engineering development should not be started until the Army has completed a system [sic] analysis and defined the characteristics of the system" (McNamara 1964).[9]

In brief, a McNamara decision to overrule the services' recommendations regarding forces and weapons implied that the civilians were better able to judge force requirements than were officers who had spent their entire professional lives developing their expertise. Every confrontation between the services and the Office of Systems Analysis exposed the nerves of military professionalism. The division of labor between civilians and the military was blurred and the special contribution of the services was challenged. As a result, the services fought the secretary not only more frequently but also more bitterly.

These results are paradoxical: although McNamara faced problems similar to those confronted by the Eisenhower administration, he apparently rejected its tactic of overruling the military's recommendations on nonmilitary grounds. Although the administration led by a war hero tended to avoid challenges to the military's claims of expertise, the administration with no such assets continually assaulted the services' presumption of exclusive competence and, as a consequence, purchased their bitterness.

The answer to this puzzle lies in the fact that McNamara's formal budgeting system, as well as the public rhetoric, prevented the exploitation of the nonmilitary argument invoked by Eisenhower. Not only did the exercise of systems analysis by OSD entail an implicit challenge to the services' raison d'être, but the administration —having deprived itself of the alternative rationale of fiscal constraints—was obliged to explicitly *invoke* the implication in order to defend its decisions. The "anti-ceilings rhetoric" of PPBS virtually required that every denial of a military request—for whatever reason—be accompanied by a challenge to the military's competence and judgment.[10]

The dilemma which McNamara confronted is best, if unintentionally, described in his own testimony before the Senate Appropriations Committee (1966, Part I, p. 367):

I believe that our Nation can afford whatever we need to spend on our military security, so there is no financial limit placed on the defense budget. To be quite frank with you, we didn't even add it up until we decided on each element of it, because it wasn't a question of 'What does it add up to?' that determines whether a particular element is to be approved, but rather whether that element supports a clear military requirement. And the $2.6 billion of fiscal year 1966 supplemental requests which I cut out [from the services' budget estimates] and the $12.9 million [sic] of fiscal year 1967 budget request which I cut out were cut out not because we couldn't afford it and not because we didn't have the financial ability to pay for it and not because of some arbitrary financial limit established in the budget but rather because those requests did not appear to support a bona fide military requirement.

McNamara's repeated public insistence that there was no ceiling on the defense budget prevented him from rejecting the services' proposals on fiscal grounds. However, he continued to face the responsibility of rejecting recommendations he believed to be unwise—as well as of conforming to the fiscal constraints which he refused to acknowledge. Since (according to McNamara's own testimony) every proposal which was militarily justifiable warranted approval, each OSD rejection of a service's recommendation unavoidably implied that the civilians had tested the military's professional judgment and had found it wanting.[11] The conclusion that the civilians were better able to judge *military* requirements than were the services themselves was inescapable. As Maxwell Taylor observed (1963–64, p. 337), there were only two possible interpretations of a rejection of military advice under such circumstances: "Either the civilian is showing dangerous overconfidence in his own military judgment or there is an incompetent military advisor." McNamara's formal budgeting system, in brief, not only increased OSD's decision-making burden but also the intensity of civil-military confrontations.

Wielding Bargaining Advantages: The Dangers of Overload

If PPBS taxed the civilians' decision-making capacities and impaired their bargaining advantages, it also contributed to the services' bargaining position. As we have seen, the services' primary bargaining advantages—especially the appearance of distinterested professionalism—depend upon their ability to make unanimous recommendations. The analysis in Chapter 3 suggested that interservice competition for resources—allocational rivalries (Downs 1967, pp. 9–10)—is an important obstacle to interservice agreement.

Allocational rivalries, however, can vary in intensity. Although the military services—like all federal agencies whose budgets are appropriated annually—always compete in principle, interservice struggles over their respective shares of the defense budget depend on the strength and visibility of the linkages between one service's budget increases and another's reductions. Differences in the budgeting systems of the Eisenhower administration and its Democratic successors produced corresponding differences in the services' incentives to *behave* like allocational rivals.

Fiscal guidance in the Eisenhower budget system made each service recognize that expansion of its activities and budget necessarily came at the expense of its sister services. By explicitly recognizing these resource limitations, it provided mechanisms for the exercise of allocational rivalries. As a result, political responsibility for choices was diffused and some of the burden for rejecting proposals was pushed down onto the services.[12] The "anti-ceilings rhetoric" of PPBS, by contrast, had the opposite effects.

It followed from McNamara's denial of a fixed amount for defense that reduction (or cancellation) of a service's program did not imply that resources had become available for reallocation. On the contrary, given the fiscal constraints within which the administration in fact operated, criticisms of a service's proposals provided opportunities to reduce total defense spending (Schlesinger 1968, pp. 11–12). Consequently, each service literally had nothing to gain by attacking a sister service's programs and actually stood a chance of being penalized (in the form of a smaller budget) for economy in its own activities. Conversely, since their proposals formally were unconstrained by a budget ceiling, the services had no incentive to accompany each new spending proposal with an equal-cost tradeoff. These circumstances encouraged what the services' interest in unanimity required: avoiding hard choices and internal dissension by asking for more of everything.[13]

Resource scarcity did not disappear during McNamara's tenure: in principle, the services remained allocational rivals. However, PPBS's ostentatious abandonment of fiscal guidance left the competition for scarce resources unstructured. Even when the services came to believe that there was a ceiling on a McNamara defense budget (Korb 1976, pp. 116–17), his budgeting system lacked any mechanism which permitted them to behave like allocational rivals. Conflict, both within and among the services, declined as the burden of setting priorities was concentrated at the OSD level. Obstacles to interservice agreement diminished and the services bargaining advantages increased correspondingly.

The formal structure and official documents of the McNamara budget cycle, which conveyed an impression of service subordination to OSD initiative and domination, further increased the concentration of political burdens on OSD. The initiative for defense programs, as well as the final decisions regarding alternatives, formally resided with the civilians. McNamara's annual posture statements to Congress were drafted in OSD. The Office of the Secretary initiated the annual budget dialogue inside the Pentagon and controlled the debate: OSD's Draft Presidential Memoranda defined the issues to be discussed while OSD's Office of Systems Analysis outlined the force structure to be supported. Thus PPBS placed the services in the ostensible position of responding to civilian initiatives and of "appealing" the decisions of civilian analysts in OSD. Notwithstanding McNamara's need—and willingness—to bargain with his uniformed subordinates, his budgeting system conveyed the *appearance* of centralized control which entailed a *real* concentration of political burdens (Hammond 1968, p. 63).[14]

In sum, PPBS—and its interaction with the participants' incentives—concentrated political responsibility for decisions on OSD as it suppressed allocational rivalries among the services. They found themselves in a stronger position vis-à-vis McNamara as the obstacles to interservice agreement diminished. At the same time, they were able to concentrate their energies on impeding or reversing uncongenial OSD decisions since they were substantially shielded from the attacks of external critics.

Wielding Bargaining Advantages:
The Limits of Functional Rivalries

McNamara surely did not intend this outcome. On the contrary, his congressional testimony suggests that he expected interservice rivalries to persist: interservice rivalries would continue, in his view, but were to be transformed from petty and debilitating bickering into a healthy and beneficial competition.

That testimony indicates that McNamara anticipated that PPBS would encourage *functional* rivalries (Downs 1967, pp. 9–10). By exploiting competition resulting from the services' overlapping responsibilities and capabilities, he hoped to inhibit the suppression of adverse information, encourage innovation, and expose defense programs to increased scrutiny. In brief, the secretary looked forward to reaping the benefits of organizational imperialism among the services.

PPBS attempted to stimulate functional rivalries by explicitly comparing military capabilities *across* services. Each of the ten defense program budget categories was composed of a large number of closely related, and frequently substitutable, "program elements." The administration announced its intention to compare proposed program elements and to choose the best alternative, regardless of which service supplied the forces. As Charles Hitch explained (U.S. Congress, Senate, 1961, Part I, p. 1025): "Decisions will depend upon the quality of the program that each service submits in comparison with other elements of the program package." Thus, by treating Navy Polaris missiles and Air Force ICBMs and manned bombers as separate program elements within the Strategic Forces Program, McNamara hoped that the Navy would view Polaris as competing for resources with comparable Air Force capabilities rather than with unrelated Navy programs as it had in the past.

In combination with the techniques of systems analysis, the PPBS practice of explicit interservice comparisons was expected to create incentives for the services to engage in substantive and analytical (if still self-interested) criticisms of one another's proposals. As McNamara forecast (U.S. Congress, Senate, 1961, Part I, p. 1196):

> The Navy will participate in a discussion of the Air Force's strategic systems. The Air Force will participate in a discussion of the Navy's strategic systems. . . . Similarly, the Navy, and Air Force and Army will join together in a consideration of the airlift, sealift, and ground requirements. . . .

The result, it was hoped, would be to generate better information and analyses of program alternatives for civilian decision-makers while simultaneously nurturing obstacles to interservice unanimity. This strategy, however, both neglected to take account of the substantial specialization which characterize the services' capabilities and failed to appreciate their incentives.

The procedure's prospects for success depended in part upon the extent of functional duplication among the services: if the degree of duplication were relatively modest, then large—and potentially important—areas of national security policy would be insulated from interservice criticism. As noted above, this in fact has been the case. Although the distinctions between the services' missions have become increasingly blurred since World War II, they have remained predominantly separate organizations with substantially unique capabilities: for the vast majority of contingencies, each service continues to be a "monopoly supplier" of military resources and capabilities.

Also, the process envisaged by McNamara assumed that overlapping capabilities would provoke organizational imperialism among the services. Organizations, however, are not aggressive "by nature." They may seek to monopolize those resources and capabilities which they deem necessary to accomplish their self-defined objectives, but their claims are not unlimited (Thompson 1961, p. 39; Holden 1966, pp. 945–46). On the contrary, the military services have repeatedly demonstrated that they will sacrifice or shun tangentially related activities in order to conserve resources and to protect their primary missions (e.g., Smith 1970, chapter 8).

Accordingly, functional duplication does not lead inexorably to functional rivalry (cf. Hirschman 1970). Under certain conditions, duplication can *mute* interservice conflict by reducing organizational interdependence. For example, interservice amity probably was advanced by the 1971 Pentagon decision to request funds for three close air-support weapons systems, one each for the Army, Air Force, and Marines. Indeed, given the services' strong interest in maintaining agreement among themselves, functional duplication can generate incentives for collusion as well as—or instead of— the seeds of competition.[15]

The formal budgeting system further reduced the benefits which the administration hoped to reap. First, the services' budget estimates continued to be prepared in the traditional line item format (which aggregated resources by service) throughout the 1960s (Crecine 1969). As a result, they had reason to doubt that resources actually were allocated on the basis of missions, without regard to which service performed them. Their skepticism only increased as experience persuaded them that McNamara's defense program decisions were only loosely related to subsequent budget decisions.

Second, the administration's "anti-ceilings rhetoric" sharply diminished any reinforcement which might have been generated by interservice allocational rivalries. On the contrary, in the absence of explicit resource constraints, service participation in the reviews of one another's programs was more an invitation to logroll than to criticize: since the system imposed few penalties on asking for more of everything, the services' interest in military consensus led them to adopt positions of mutual support rather than of mutual criticism. By the FY 1966 budget, the Joint Chiefs unanimously supported the Air Force's request for a follow-on manned bomber, the

Army's request for ABM, and the Navy's request for additional nuclear submarines (Korb 1970).

Conclusion

PPBS in McNamara's Pentagon produced a number of unintended —and undesirable—consequences. They were perhaps best characterized by the administration's inattention to the incentives of its uniformed subordinates and by its insensitivity to its own vulnerability to overload. It apparently overestimated its ability to compel compliance from the military services and badly miscalculated the implications of ignoring fiscal constraints. The result was an administration characterized by a hard-working and aggressive civilian leadership in national security policy but one whose impact on outputs was substantially indistinguishable from that of its predecessors.

7

Military Subordinates as Policy Allies
Eliciting Compliance

Our analysis of defense budgets and budget systems has emphasized the conflicts between the administration's policy preferences and those of the military services. Accordingly, the discussion has concentrated on the problem of prevailing—with the attendant connotations of struggle and coercion. This emphasis, however, has neglected the potential to reduce the frequency of deliberate noncompliance by means of persuasion. That is, compliance may be elicited as well as compelled.

Improving Compliance: The "Personnel Approach"
Clearly, the president's persuasive task would be eased to the extent that his subordinates were predisposed to support his proposals. To this end, presidents have relied on their extensive formal authority to pick and choose their senior uniformed subordinates. The postwar record reveals persistent efforts to fill the highest military positions with officers who would advance the administration's national security policies. In particular, postwar presidents have attempted to increase the number of unanimous JCS endorsements by exploiting the authority of the commander-in-chief to replace personnel at the highest level and to alter their formal status. In brief, presidents have adopted a "personnel approach" to eliciting compliance from the services.

Two complementary maneuvers have been employed. First, the incumbent Chiefs have been replaced with officers who were believed to possess policy preferences which were more compatible with those of the administration. Second, efforts have been made to redistribute formal authority and the symbols of military expertise in favor of positions whose occupants were believed to be more dependable and sympathetic. The most visible example of this campaign has been the elevation of the chairman to *primus inter pares* (Lucas and Dawson 1974, p. 65).

Eisenhower (1963, pp. 447–48), acknowledged that a paramount defense policy objective was to minimize service partisanship within the JCS—to get it to speak with one voice (presumably in support of the administration's programs).[1] Accordingly, one of the first actions of the incoming administration was to replace the Chiefs who had served under Truman.[2]

Eisenhower gave special attention to the selection of a new chairman who would be an enthusiastic spokesman for the new strategic doctrine.[3] Having found his man in Admiral Arthur Radford, Eisenhower endeavored to improve his status. By virtue of the 1953 Reorganization of the Defense Department, the position of the chairman was strengthened, especially by placing an enlarged Joint Staff under his control (Ries 1964, pp. 154–55). The chairman's new status also was enhanced by more symbolic gestures. For example, the chairman regularly attended the meetings of the National Security Council, ordinarily unaccompanied by the other Chiefs (Jackson 1965, p. 122). Taylor (1960, p. 109) nicely summarizes this administration campaign to make the chairman the most visible symbol of disinterested military expertise:

> The Chairman accompanies the Secretary to many important meetings at home and abroad, where he serves as his principal military adviser. The Chairman soon becomes identified in the mind of the Secretary, and indeed elsewhere *in and out of the government, as the authentic voice of the armed services.* It is not uncommon to confuse the views of the Chairman with those of the corporate body of the Chiefs and to attribute mistakenly to the Chiefs the personal position of the Chairman. [Emphasis added]

At least with regard to tactics for staffing the JCS and directing attention to a single, dependably supportive military advisor, the Kennedy administration emulated its predecessor. Like Eisenhower, Kennedy wanted Chiefs whose policy preferences complemented his own and who would support him publicly (and not betray him privately). According to Theodore Sorensen (1966, p. 685): "Compatibility with the President's thinking was as important in the Joint Chiefs, Kennedy believed, as in the head of any civilian department." Kennedy, however, was unwilling to pay the political price of replacing the incumbent Chiefs with his own choices. Instead, he continued to direct attention away from the Joint Chiefs of Staff as a corporate military advisor.

Since one of the last acts of the Eisenhower administration was to appoint a new JCS chairman, Lyman Lemnitzer had virtually his entire term left to serve when Kennedy entered the White House. The new president temporarily resolved this problem by an informal, but de facto, circumvention of the Joint Chiefs of Staff. He recalled Maxwell Taylor from retirement and named him "Military Representative." In a gesture of considerable symbolic significance, Taylor's office was physically located in the White House while, of course, the JCS continued to operate across the Potomac.

From that position, Taylor could operate much as did Radford vis-à-vis the president's constituencies outside the executive branch, as an articulate and enthusiastic general officer certifying the military wisdom of Kennedy's national security programs. When Lemnitzer's term expired in 1962, Taylor replaced him as chairman and continued his Radford-like function from the Pentagon.

It is difficult to evaluate the overall impact of these presidential strategies which assume the existence of important individual differences among the military officers' policy preferences. The record, however, suggests that the results of these efforts are mixed at best. Notwithstanding his wholesale replacement of the incumbent Chiefs, Eisenhower nevertheless experienced many of the same problems with his own appointees to the JCS. For example, both Army Chief of Staff Ridgway and Chief of Naval Operations Carney disputed the fundamental assumption which underpinned the New Look by *publicly* denying that the development of tactical nuclear weapons implied reduced manpower requirements.[4]

Eisenhower's choices to fill the senior JCS position also exhibited some variation in their conception of the chairman's proper role and function. Radford rejected both a role which would make him the Chiefs' emissary to the administration and a role in which he would function as a broker-conciliator within the JCS seeking to construct compromises and to promote consensus among the Chiefs. Instead, Taylor wrote (1960, p. 110), "the Chairman has come to be a sort of party whip, charged with conveying the official line to the Chiefs in the hope and expectation that they will be guided thereby in their actions." Nathan Twining, on the other hand, adopted a more neutral role as chairman and, according to Taylor, was "much less a partisan of the official line than [was] Admiral Radford" (Taylor 1960, p. 110).

The chairmen selected by the Democrats displayed similar contrasts. At least some of the Chiefs viewed Maxwell Taylor "as a representative of the administration" while he served as chairman.[5] However, General Earle Wheeler, a Taylor protégé who succeeded to the position of chairman, increasingly functioned as the Chiefs' representative and lobbyist in the administration, disagreeing publicly with administration policy (Henry 1971).

The record thus suggests that the military "personnel policy" of postwar administrations has been an inadequate and undependable instrument to secure full and faithful subordinate compliance. In part, the policy's shortcomings may be attributed to presidents' reluctance to exercise their formal authority to replace incumbent Chiefs. Outgoing presidents have tended to saddle their successors by making JCS appointments during the last year of their terms. Except for Eisenhower, however, incoming presidents have permitted the holdover Chiefs to complete their appointments rather than pay the political price of replacing them (Korb 1976, p. 31). Also, presidents undoubtedly have been hampered by a lack of personal familiarity with the candidates and have committed errors of judgment in selecting their Chiefs.

The central obstacles, however, are systemic. Every senior military officer is the product of a closed personnel system which has shaped his perspectives throughout his adult life. Every prospective Chief of Staff, moreover, is subject to organizational constraints on his discretion and behavior. As a result, any president, of necessity, is severely limited in his choice of senior military advisors. They, in turn, are severely limited in their ability to command support from their services. JCS chairmen, who lack direct ties to any service, are even more limited.

In brief, the shortcomings of the "personnel approach" confirm the conclusions of our analysis of organizational behavior: efforts to persuade professional officers—or any other career bureaucrats—to "rise above" their organizational concerns are certain to be strenuous and likely to be futile. The president instead must take account of an ineradicable "parochialism" and harness it to his purposes. He must recognize and exploit the bureaucratic processes he cannot overcome.

The military services, however, hold the promise of being repositories of support for administration defense policies as well as being sources of opposition. Their organizational complexity yields a diversity of potential policy alternatives; the clash of policy preferences not only occurs between the civilians and the military but also within and among the services themselves.

One strategy available to the president is to exploit any islands of support within the services in order to reduce the probability of noncompliance. He benefits from the fact that virtually any administration defense policy "initiative" is likely to converge with the incentives and priorities of at least some groups within the military at the same time that it conflicts with the interests of others in uniform.[6] His task is to discover military subordinates within the services who—for their own reasons—endorse his choices, and to strengthen their bargaining advantages vis-à-vis their uniformed colleagues in intraservice debates.[7] For this strategy to succeed, however, the processes by which the services establish priorities among their nominal responsibilities first must be understood (cf. Allison and Szanton 1976).

Setting Service Priorities: Organizational Parochialism and Responsiveness

It is more fruitful to consider a military service's view of its distinctive mission and objectives—what Halperin (1974, p. 28) has termed its "organizational essence"—as a constraint on alternative definitions of its priorities than as a unique and well-defined set of activities (White 1974). For example, the Air Force is responsible for the development and deployment of military aerospace capabilities. That mission, however, does not specify whether the Air Force should emphasize long-range or short-range aircraft, whether its role is predominantly tactical or strategic, or what the appropriate relationship is between manned aircraft and unmanned missiles.[8]

The range of roles and missions, within and across services, is a gauge of the president's opportunities to find support for his policies among the military. Like those of any large-scale organization, however, a military service's potential functions exceed its capacity and its resources: it cannot embrace all of its roles and missions equally. Priorities must be set: some activities must be considered to be more tangential as certain tasks are identified as fundamental to the service's self-defined purposes.

The diversity of a service's capabilities is reflected in the technical specialization of its members as well as in its organizational structure, for example, "branches" in the Army and "commands" in the Air Force. As a consequence, each of the service's functions tends to have organizationally based advocates.

Since the services are substantially hierarchical in fact as well as in form, the distribution of those advocates in the ranks of the senior officers is both a symbol and a source of the relative priorities among a service's roles and missions (Huntington 1961a, p. 406). These senior officers can and do give orders to those in the ranks below with the well-founded expectation that those orders will be carried out. For the reasons given in Chapter 2, those who dominate the senior ranks not only can speak for their particular intraservice component but can claim—with justice—to represent the entire service.[9] In brief, the operative goals of a military service are what its most senior officers say they are.[10]

This process by which a service gives operational content to its official goals, a process characterized by a clash among intraservice advocates over priorities, is the manifestation or organizational parochialism which the president must confront and exploit. The search for convergence between the operative goals of the services and the administration's national security policy preferences directs attention to (a) the factors leading to an intraservice group's dominance and subsequent displacement and (b) the ability of the administration to influence those variables.

Perrow (1961, pp. 854–57) has argued that the specific challenges and problems generated by an organization's environment will determine which of its subunits will prevail: when the organization's membership perceives that a particular faction is best equipped to deal with organization-wide problems or opportunities, "a presumptive basis for control or domination by the group" is created, and that subunit rises to organizational dominance. This controlling group shapes the operational content of the organization's goals, based upon the perspectives and priorities spawned by its members' professional backgrounds. Intraorganizational groups rise and fall in influence as the organization's problems and opportunities change. The operational content of the organization's goals changes accordingly. Perrow argues, in short, that relations among an organization's participants are responsive to changes in its environment and that the composition of its leadership and its self-defined priorities are a function of that environment.

Perrow's analysis parallels both Vincent Davis's description of Navy strategic planning for the postwar period (1966) and Perry Smith's discussion of related efforts by the Air Force (1970). These authors conclude that the content of the strategic doctrine promoted by each service was a reflection of the distribution of influence among intraservice groups. Alterations in the intraservice distribution of influence (and corresponding shifts in doctrinal emphasis), in turn, are attributed to changes in the services' environment. That is, these case studies explain variation in the composition of the senior officer corps by reference to the services' responsiveness to a changing environment.

They agree that the strategic environment, for example, the projected behavior of potential foreign adversaries, had only a modest impact on the services' behavior. Rather, the environmental stimuli toward which their strategic planning efforts were directed were overwhelmingly *domestic* in origin and were predominantly defined in *organizational* terms. Smith argues (1970, p. 14): "The focus of attention for the postwar planners . . . was planning for Air

Force independence from the United States Army." Davis (1966, pp. 155–56) characterizes the Navy's efforts in strikingly similar terms:

> The political fight with the War Department and, more particularly, with the Air Force soon dominated the Navy men's every consideration. Their responses to this political struggle—which they sincerely believed to be a fight for the very survival of their service—thus provided the context for all remaining decisions about the postwar Navy.

Declining manpower levels and shrinking defense budgets were the features of the postwar domestic environment to which both services were responding. The delivery of nuclear weapons by aircraft was the only mission which promised to generate sufficient enthusiasm and support in the administration and Congress (Davis 1966, p. 196). For the Navy, these circumstances posed a serious threat to its organizational well-being. For the Army Air Force (AAF), the situation was an opportunity for organizational autonomy. Both services responded by emphasizing the nuclear airpower mission and their distinctive capabilities to fulfiill that role.

As suggested by Perrow, this environment strengthened the position of certain intraservice groups and gave them a presumptive claim to leadership of the entire service. Smith observes (1970, p. 27) that the cause—and bargaining advantages—of the advocates of strategic airpower, the "bomber generals," were promoted within the Air Force because "the doctrine and decisiveness of strategic bombardment in future warfare were inextricably tied to the AAF case for autonomy." Likewise in the Navy, the "battleship admirals" gave way to the "aviator admirals." As Davis explains (1966, p. 149): "If the Navy was going to advertise that the heart of modern sea forces was aviation, then it would have to act accordingly, and this in effect assured the success of the naval aviators' bid for the dominant position in the postwar Navy."

Thus, the priorities among roles and missions set by the services themselves, and the policies they were eager to advocate, were conditioned by threats and opportunities they perceived in their organizational environment. Specifically, the *strategic preferences of elected politicians*, and the *allocation of budgetary resources* in a manner consistent with these preferences, were identified by Davis and Smith as the origins of the changing distribution of influence within the services and the defense policies advocated by them.

If their findings have broader applicability, an administration may be able to increase the probability that "like-minded" officers will be promoted to senior ranks at the expense of those with contrary perspectives and priorities. This potential rests on the hypothesized responsiveness of the military services qua organizations to changes in their environment, and on that environment's susceptibility to manipulation by the incumbent administration. These hypotheses can be tested by means of time-series data on the promotion probabilities of selected intraservice groups.

The Promotions Process as a Mechanism of Organizational Responsiveness

Data are available on promotions in the Navy and the Air Force.[11] As would be expected, the probability that an officer will be promoted is inversely related to rank. Junior officers are promoted virtually as a matter of routine. As Chu and White (1975, p. 258) have remarked about the operation of the services' "up or out" promotion systems: "in the early years of an officer's career, it is mostly 'up' and rarely 'out.' " Indeed, their data indicate that most officers will reach the grade of lieutenant colonel/commander before they retire with twenty years of service. Consequently, interesting differences among the promotion probabilities of various intraservice groups are unlikely to emerge below this grade.

Promotions to very senior grades also have been excluded from the analysis. The small number of cases involved increases the difficulty of distinguishing idiosyncratic factors from generalized patterns. Unlike other promotions, moreover, those of three- and four-star rank are not made by service boards. Promotions to these grades instead are related to the specific assignments being filled (Chu and White, 1975, p. 265). Finally, civilian attempts to intervene in the selection process are most likely to occur at very senior grades.[12] While such administration efforts testify to the importance attached to the staffing of senior military positions, it confounds an analysis of a service's autonomous response to changes in its environment.

These considerations suggest that an analysis of lower-ranking general (flag) officers is a fruitful starting point. Accordingly, annual Navy selections for promotion to "lower-half" rear admiral were analyzed.[13] In recent years, 25 to 30 rear admirals have been selected annually from among the 200 to 300 captains considered for promotion. Since comparable Air Force data on selection to brigadier general were not available, promotions to the next highest grade—colonel—were analyzed. In recent years, 300 to 1,000 officers have been selected annually for promotion to colonel from among the 4,000 to 7,000 eligible lieutenant colonels.

The Navy data (for the period FY 1956 to FY 1971) permit only one distinction: rated officers (those qualified for flying duties) versus other Unrestricted Line Officers. (Officers in the "surface Navy" are not distinguished from submariners within his residual category). Air Force data for the same time-period likewise distinguish between rated and nonrated officers. In addition, Air Force promotion data for the period FY 1954 to FY 1971 are categorized in terms of the officers' intraservice assignments at the time of consideration for promotion. Several of these intraservice commands and operating agencies approximate the informal interest groups within the Air Force.[14]

Although the promotion procedures for each service vary in specific detail, there is sufficient similarity in the general process to permit a single description and comparative analysis.[15] The number of officers to be selected for promotion to the next highest grade is based on predictions of the vacancies likely to occur during the next year. The officers formally eligible to be considered for promotion are determined on the basis of a seniority criterion. These officers are said to be within the promotion "zone."[16]

Selection boards nominally choose officers for promotion on the basis of their individual qualifications and performance, that is, the "best" officers are selected. The promotions process, however, unavoidably delegates considerable discretion to the selection board members who make the actual promotion choices. This discretion results in large measure from an inability to translate imprecise conceptions about the service's ultimate purposes into operational and nondiscretionary criteria. As a result, the relative qualifications of the officers under consideration are determined by the professional intuitive judgment of their seniors on the selection board, operating within the boundaries demarcated by the formal rules of the system.[17]

There are no acknowledged quotas based on intraservice specialties and skills: there is nothing in the formal selection process which requires a particular intraservice group, for example, Air Force bomber pilots, to receive a specified share of the promotions. On the contrary, the statutes regulating the selection process prohibit reference to the "needs of the service" when comparing the qualifications of officers under consideration. Consequently, any trends in promotion probabilities are not simply artifacts of official directives or administrative procedures.

On the other hand, the absence of objective criteria for determining qualifications allows for the operation of unacknowledged decision rules in the selection process. In particular, it is likely that the selection board's evaluation of an officer's qualifications encompasses his prospective contribution to the service. That estimate, in turn, is inextricably connected with the board members' perceptions of the tasks and problems confronting the service. That is, the priorities held by the board members, as well as their understanding of their service's future needs and opportunities, may be reflected in their selection choices among intraservice groups (Feld 1967). Changes in the relative success of intraservice groups in achieving promotions to senior rank would be one measure of the service's reevaluation of its needs in response to perceived changes in its environment.

Patterns of Promotion in the Navy and Air Force

Since the pool of eligible officers is not equally divided among the various intraservice communities, each faction's share of the total annual promotions is a misleading measure of success. Instead, the annual promotions drawn from each group were related to that faction's representation among the officers considered for selection by computing its "promotion opportunity ratio" (POR) as follows:

$$POR_i = \frac{(S_i/C_i)}{(S_j/C_j)}$$

where:

POR_i = the promotion opportunity ratio for intraservice group$_i$ (relative to group$_j$)

S_i = the number of officers in group$_i$ selected for promotion

C_i = the number of officers in group$_i$ considered for promotion

S_j = the number of officers in group$_j$ selected for promotion

C_j = the number of officers in group$_j$ considered for promotion

If the proportion of eligible officers in group$_i$ who are promoted is equal to the proportion of eligible officers in group$_j$ who are promoted, then $R_i = 1.00$. If the officers in group$_i$ stand a relatively better chance of promotion than those in group$_j$, then $R_i > 1.00$. If the opportunities for promotion in group$_i$ are lower than those

in group$_j$, then $R_i < 1.00$. The PORs calculated for selected intraservice groups in the Navy and the Air Force are shown in table 21.

If the actual operation of the selection process has conformed to
the impression conveyed by the formal rules, that is, if knowledge
of the intraservice group membership of an officer does not improve
predictions of his promotion opportunity, then the PORs should
vary around 1.00 and should be uncorrelated with time. Alterna-

Table 21. Promotion Opportunity Ratios, Selected Intraservice
Groups

Fiscal Year	Navy rated captains (relative to nonrated)	Air Force rated lt. colonels (relative to nonrated)	Air Force SAC (relative to "Limited War Command")	SAC-secondary zone (relative to "Limited War Command")
1954	—	—	3.23	—
1955	—	—	2.95	—
1956	2.39	3.00	1.67	—
1957	2.38	3.30	2.46	—
1958	2.04	2.76	1.24	—
1959	1.93	1.93	1.43	—
1960	1.87	—	—	—
1961	1.71	—	—	—
1962	1.43	1.10	1.20	1.03
1963	1.52	0.81	1.63	2.53
1964	1.40	1.07	1.45	—
1965	1.58	1.31	1.32	0.80
1966	1.66	1.78	0.95	1.13
1967	1.27	1.63	0.97	0.43
1968	1.14	1.41	0.85	0.41
1969	0.94	1.09	0.64	0.18
1970	1.03	1.60	0.60	0.35
1971	0.82	1.14	0.88	0.31

Sources: Computed from data supplied by Navy Department and
Department of the Air Force.

tively, a group's promotion opportunity ratios may be significantly
different from, but approximately parallel to, a "fair share" 1.00
line over time. These results might reflect the experience of an
intraservice community which had been consistently rewarded or
penalized throughout the time period. Such findings would suggest
either that the internal structure of the service has been unresponsive to changes in its environment or that its environment has not
undergone important changes. Finally, the annual PORs may be

correlated with time. This trend would be consistent with an organizational response to changes in its environment which included an internal redistribution of bargaining advantages and the ascendancy of a new intraservice group.

The promotion opportunity ratios for naval aviators (relative to other unrestricted line captains) for selection to rear admiral are shown in figure 1.[18] A clear trend is discernible: the chances that a naval aviator would be promoted to flag grade have declined steadily since the 1950s. During the early part of the period, aviators were about twice as likely as nonrated captains to be promoted to rear admiral. By the end of the 1960s, aviators experienced approximately the same probability of promotion as the balance of unrestricted line captains. The passage of time—or whatever variables were changing during the period—accounts for approximately 90 percent of the variance in the aviators' promotion opportunity ratios ($r = -0.95$, $p = .01$).

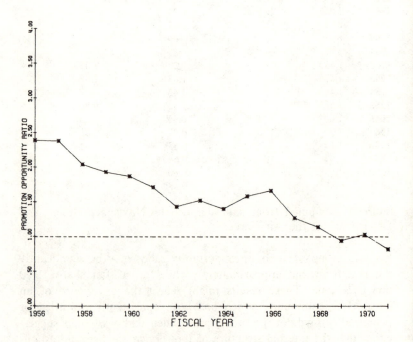

Fig. 1. Naval aviators' promotion opportunity ratios (relative to nonrated captains)

These results suggest that the aviators' rise to dominance of the postwar Navy, detailed by Davis (1966), continued into the 1950s. During this period, the Navy's priorities among its potential roles and missions—and the defense policy alternatives it advocated—were substantially those dictated by the needs of naval aviation. The aviators' declining PORs indicate that their domination has been successfully challenged in recent years by other intraservice groups. The range of policies which the Navy will support with enthusiasm has expanded accordingly.

The promotion opportunity ratios for rated lieutenant colonels in the Air Force (relative to other nonrated line officers) for selection to colonel are shown in figure 2. The PORs of rated officers in the Air Force also have declined over time, although the trend is neither as consistent nor as well-defined as in the Navy: about half of the change in their PORs can be explained by the passage of time ($r = -0.72$, $p = .01$).

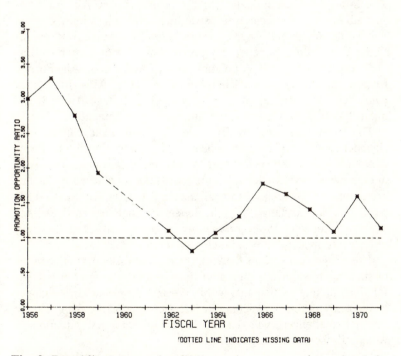

Fig. 2. Rated lieutenant colonels' promotion opportunity ratios (relative to nonrated officers)

The Air Force of the 1950s was overwhelmingly dominated by pilots, and, at least prior to the introduction of ballistic missiles, there was nearly universal intraservice agreement that the service's raison d'être was to fly aircraft in combat. Although a decline in the pilots' promotion opportunity ratios coincided with changes in technology and new missions (ICBMs, space boosters) which were less related to piloting manned aircraft, the Air Force remains very much a flying organization (Margiotta 1975, p. 43). It is, after all, the *Air* Force.[19]

As was seen in Chapter 2, the Air Force's internal structure has become increasingly differentiated over time. Since several Air Force commands approximate intraservice communities, the promotion opportunity ratios for lieutenant colonels assigned to different commands parallel the relative success experienced by these intraservice groups. In particular, the distinction between *strategic* offensive warfare missions and *limited* warfare missions is reflected in the different responsibilities of particular Air Force commands. The Strategic Air Command (SAC) bears primary Air Force responsibility for strategic war capabilities and operations. Several Air Force commands share responsibility for limited war operations. The three commands composed primarily of fighter and attack aircraft—Tactical Air Command (TAC); U.S. Air Forces, Europe (USAFE); and Pacific Air Forces (PACAF)—have been combined for purposes of analysis with the Military Airlift Command (MAC) into a synthetic "limited war command."

The promotion opportunity ratios for lieutenant colonels assigned to SAC (relative to officers assigned to the "limited war command") are shown in figure 3. The trend resembles that seen in the case of the naval aviators: the passage of time accounts for approximately 75 percent of the variance in SAC's PORs ($r = -0.85$, $p = .01$). By the late 1960s, lieutenant colonels assigned to SAC stood a somewhat lower probability of being promoted than did officers assigned to the "limited war command."[20]

These high correlations between the promotion opportunity ratios of major intraservice groups and time support the hypothesis that relations among participants within the services respond to changes in their environment: reigning intraservice groups are displaced by internal challengers who can better exploit the new situation in which the service finds itself.

Exploiting Organizational Responsiveness: Strategic Doctrine
These findings lead to the question of what kinds of changes in the environment—which are susceptible to manipulation by the ci-

vilian administration—can be associated with the observed trends. The case studies of the postwar Navy (Davis 1966) and Air Force (Smith 1970) suggested that the priorities among roles and missions implied by the administration's strategic doctrine determined which intraservice groups would predominate. This explanation also would account for the observed changes in promotion opportunity ratios during the 1950s and 1960s.

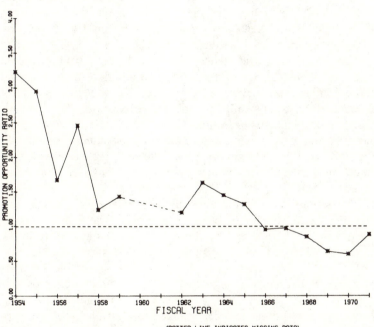

Fig. 3. Air Force SAC promotion opportunity ratios (relative to "Limited War Command")

The relationship between shifts in strategic doctrine and changes in PORs is particularly clear in the changing promotion prospects for officers assigned to the Strategic Air Command. As we have seen, the Eisenhower administration's New Look in defense policy —and its hallmark of massive retaliation—emphasized strategic airpower at the expense of conventional capabilities. At the *inter*-service level, this policy benefited the Air Force while it penalized the Army.

At the *intra*service level, the same administration policy created presumptions which conferred considerable bargaining advantages on the Air Force group whose training and professional perspectives most closely approximated the administration's priorities. When massive retaliation was the backbone of national defense, the promotion opportunity ratios for lieutenant colonels assigned to SAC were considerably in excess of 1.00. The Eisenhower administration, in turn, faced a frequently too enthusiastic proponent of its early defense policies as it searched for support and compliance from its military subordinates.

SAC's PORs declined as the administration's doctrine underwent redefinition. The evolution of the doctrine culminated in what has been dubbed the "New New Look" (Huntington 1961a, pp. 88–113). In apparent acknowledgement of the growing Soviet strategic nuclear capabilities, the second Eisenhower administration placed relatively less stress on decisive strategic airstrikes and somewhat more emphasis on the concept of deterrence at various levels of conflict. Eisenhower's shift in emphasis weakened the Strategic Air Command's claim to leadership within the Air Force. Public pronouncements of the reformulated doctrine by administration officials occurred in late 1956 (Quarles 1956) and 1957 (Dulles 1957). Soon thereafter, the promotion opportunity ratios for officers assigned to SAC begin to decline more sharply.

The Kennedy administration's doctrine of flexible response further decreased reliance on strategic airpower. The delivery of nuclear weapons by manned bombers occupied a low priority in the new order. (Indeed, the importance attached to survivable "second-strike" capabilities occasionally implied that vulnerable bombers were somewhat worse than redundant.) The promotion prospects for officers assigned to the "limited war command" steadily improved as the administration's emphasis on less-than-strategic capabilities increased. By the middle 1960s, lieutenant colonels in SAC were relatively disadvantaged in choices of the annual selection boards, especially in selections from the secondary zone.

The relationship between changes in strategic doctrine and the naval aviator's promotion opportunity ratios is more complex. As we have seen, the naval aviators' postwar rise to dominance was a consequence of the Navy's search for a role in the mission to which the administration had assigned the highest priority. The strategic objectives of carrier-based airpower in the Navy became virtually indistinguishable from those of the Strategic Air Command (Davis 1966, p. 228), and the naval aviators' PORs were substantially greater than those for other captains of the unrestricted line during the 1950s.

The Kennedy administration's quest for a secure second-strike strategic capability, however, left the aviators vulnerable to the claims of the submariners with responsibility for the Polaris missile force. The administration's search for military options in addition to strategic nuclear power also increased the importance of functions performed by other intra-Navy groups and, consequently, strengthened the claim of these groups to participate in defining the Navy's priorities. In brief, the future of the Navy ceased to be synonymous with the success of the naval aviators during the 1960s. Thus, the naval aviators confronted the same situation as the bomber pilots in SAC: technological developments had altered the capabilities required to perform their primary function while changes in official defense policy had diminished the relative importance of their mission.

Unlike the bomber pilots, however, the naval aviators were able to reduce their losses by modifying the basis of their claimed contribution to the Navy's organizational well-being. The carrier admirals began to embrace the doctrine of flexible response and to emphasize the unique contributions which carrier-based airpower could make to limited war operations (Hunter 1973, pp. 195–96). For example, in an effort to protect their share of the Navy budget during the Vietnam War—and their influence within the service—the naval aviators stressed the importance of the air war in the north for the outcome of the conflict. Granted that premise, it was easy to demonstrate the unique "contribution" of carrier-based airpower, especially to the other intraservice communities (Deagle 1975, p. 427). Although the naval aviators' PORs suffered the same pattern of decline as those of SAC, such adaptability—and opportunities—reduced its magnitude: by the late 1960s naval aviators were selected for promotion to rear admiral in approximately the same proportion as were other captains in the unrestricted line.

Exploiting Organizational Responsiveness: Defense Budgets

The shifting challenges presented by the services' organizational environment were not confined to mere policy pronouncements by the incumbent administration. As we have seen, the Eisenhower administration, like its Democratic successors, exploited the budgeting process to allocate resources in support of its strategic preferences. That is, more funds were available for some defense programs and activities than for others: the threats and opportunities in the services' environment were manifest in the distribution of the administration's defense budget among the roles and missions proffered by the services.

Each military service, accordingly, confronted the task of reconciling its preferences with the funding priorities of the administration. The services had little choice but to respond to the preference ordering of the administration, since the administration controlled the budget. This was the self-interested argument, which General Medaris used on his Army colleagues in 1954 as he tried to secure additional resources for his missile program:

> You're fighting a losing game. If you put all your energy and effort into justifying these conventional weapons and ammunition even though I know we need them, I think you are going to get very little money of any kind. . . . If you increase your demands for guided missiles, I think there is a fair chance you can get a decent budget. Why don't you accentuate the positive and go with that which is popular, since you cannot get the other stuff anyway? [Quoted in Huntington 1961a, p. 418]

An Air Force colonel suggested that the same incentives operated during McNamara's tenure. He explained that his service expanded its budget request for the Tactical Air Command during the 1960s when "the Air Force discovered that's where the money is" (confidential interview).

Melvin Laird adopted a strategem which attempted to exploit these incentives in order to increase the services' support for withdrawal from Vietnam. Before Laird took office, many of the costs of the war were treated as increments to be added to the funds devoted to the services' base-line forces. This arrangement meant that cost of military operations in Southeast Asia simply increased the defense budget total. As secretary of defense, Laird reduced the Vietnam-related budget planning assumptions (e.g., level of operations, duration of conflict). His "fiscal guidance" to the services (the budget ceiling) was reduced accordingly. This change meant that the longer the U.S. remained militarily active in Southeast Asia, the greater the prospects that the services would pay for the war out of funds intended for their base-line forces. Military resistance to withdrawing from Vietnam—Laird's objective—diminished somewhat as a result (confidential interview).

The program budget format introduced by McNamara permits a systematic test of the relationship suggested by these examples. That format aggregates budget resources in terms of defense programs which approximate the missions performed by the military services. A historical reconstruction of the Eisenhower administration's defense budgets since FY 1956 in program budget categories also is available.[21] This means that, for the period FY 1956 to FY 1971, changes in the allocation of resources among military missions can be compared with changes in the promotion opportunities experienced by various intraservice groups in the Navy and Air Force. If the intraservice distribution of bargaining advantages is responsive to changes in the service's environment, variations in the distribution of the budget should be systematically reflected in corresponding changes in the PORs of the affected groups.

Program I of the defense budget includes those resources devoted to Strategic Forces. Program II contains the funds that support General Purpose Forces (those for less-than-strategic nuclear war). Another budget program, Airlift and Sealift, reflects the cost of providing mobility to the General Purpose Forces. The combination of the latter two programs therefore approximates the sum of the defense budget resources directed at the limited war mission. The ratio of the Program I budget to this limited war budget reflects the relative budgetary emphasis devoted to these missions.

The correlation between the strategic/limited war budget ratio and the Strategic Air Command's POR (lagged two years) was $r = 0.91$ ($p = .01$). That is, changes in the relative budgetary emphasis devoted to strategic missions accounted for about 83 percent of the change in SAC's PORs.[22] Even more striking than this strong statistical relationship, however, is the close correspondence between the year-to-year changes in these two measures. In all but two cases, between-year increases and decreases in the strategic/limited war budget ratio were followed by respective increases and decreases in SAC's PORs (lagged two years). In brief, the promotion opportunity measure and the budgetary measure show a strong tendency to "zig" and "zag" together.

As expected, there is a weaker relationship between the naval aviators' PORs and the relative budgetary emphasis placed on strategic and on limited warfare missions. The correlation between the naval aviators' PORs (lagged two years) and the strategic/limited war budget ratio was $r = 0.82$ ($p = .01$): the shifting distribution of budget funds among broad warfare missions accounts for about two-thirds of the variation observed in the Navy PORs. The year-to-year changes in the two measures also do not track as well: in five cases out of thirteen, the direction of change in one measure was the opposite of that in the other. Although these relationships are not as striking as those in the Air Force, the general outlines nevertheless are similar: as less of the budget was devoted to missions to which the naval aviators could make unique claims, their promotion chances decreased relative to other unrestricted line captains.

In sum, shifts in the defense budget among the major military missions were closely associated with changes in the promotion opportunity ratios of the intraservice groups with predominant responsibility for strategic and limited war. Lagging PORs yields a temporal sequence which is consistent with the causal inferences drawn above: promotion opportunity ratios *respond to* changes in strategic doctrine operationalized in terms of budgetary allocations.

Conclusion

The analysis of the intraservice promotions process suggests that an administration's search for compliance need not be confined to strategies for *prevailing*. The data on promotion probabilities indicate the feasibility of indirectly *eliciting* compliance by manipulating the services' perceptions of their organizational problems and opportunities (cf. Lindblom 1968, p. 97).

As the perceived "needs of the service" change, the dominant intraservice group's presumption to leadership can be successfully challenged from within—notwithstanding its domination of the senior ranks and annual selection boards. Changes in the service's environment, which are susceptible to manipulation by the incumbent administration, reallocate bargaining advantages within the service. The challenging faction will argue to its fellow officers—including those in the dominant group—that the latter's continued domination in the face of new conditions may result in a military service which the president does not need and will not support. Without that support, and in the presence of organizational competitors always hungry for scarce resources and eager to expand their roles and missions, the outcome could be organizational stagnation.

Such arguments are likely to be persuasive to participants who, like the "battleship admirals" in the postwar Navy, attach a high value to the "good of the service." The service's response to its changed environment is reflected in shifts in the promotion probabilities of various intraservice groups, aggressively sought by the challengers but ultimately accepted by the dominant group (cf. March 1962, pp. 674–75). The transition may be neither gracious nor swift, but the data suggest that a military service—acting in its organizational self-interest—will narrow the gap between its understanding of its responsibilities and the president's view of his needs.

There are important constraints on the ability of the administration to induce compliance in this manner. The range of alternative roles and missions advocated by competing intraservice communities substantially defines the administration's opportunities for support. Accordingly, there may be no group whose professional perspectives converge with the administration's defense policies: although an already existing competitive relationship may be exploitable, it is less clear how one can be created. Moreover, there are some potential actions (for example, uncompensated budget and personnel reductions) which are likely to provoke unanimous resistance, regardless of the distribution of professional perspectives and the range of policy preferences within the services. Finally, the promotions process may produce policy allies too slowly to meet the president's needs—and short time-horizons. In the extreme, the results might parallel those mythical generals who always prepare to fight the last war, that is, a dominant intraservice coalition which is responsive to the *previous* administration's national security problems and purposes.

Nevertheless, the analysis does suggest the potential for increasing the convergence between the administration's policies and the services' preferences. A president can do more than compel compliance. By utilizing his formal authority to allocate budget resources in support of his policy preferences, he can *move* the services' definitions of their tasks and responsibilities closer to his own.[23] By exploiting the internal dynamics of the services, he can promote the cause—and the influence—of like-minded advocates within the services. He can increase the probability that those officers who—for their own reasons—share his objectives can capture control of their organization and place it in the service of their mutually compatible goals.

Appendix: Transformation of Navy Promotion Data

During the period under investigation, there was a change in the criterion according to which data on Navy captains eligible for selection to rear admiral were reported. Prior to FY 1965, all captains within specified "year groups" (the year in which the commission was awarded) were considered eligible (although in fact few if any rear admirals were selected from among the most junior year-groups). Beginning in FY 1965, captains were groups in terms of zones, that is, above the zone, within the zone, and below the zone. Virtually all selections came from below the zone, but below-the-zone eligibles were unreported from FY 1965 to FY 1970. This change in reporting promotion statistics meant that, beginning in FY 1965, a relatively smaller number of captains were reported as eligible for selection. It therefore was necessary to transform one subset of the data to conform with the other.

The information which related year-groups to zone boundaries was not available. (The relationship would not have been perfect in any case since zone boundaries may split year-groups.) It was decided to estimate which year-groups would have been reported in the "captains eligible" statistics if the reporting rules from FY 1965 to FY 1970 had applied throughout the period. The shape of the POR trend based on unadjusted data implied that a linear transformation would be appropriate. Accordingly, correlating the unadjusted data with the transformed data would indicate the adequacy of the transformation criterion. In addition, the data for FY 1971 fortuitously permit an application of the transformation criterion and a comparison of the results.

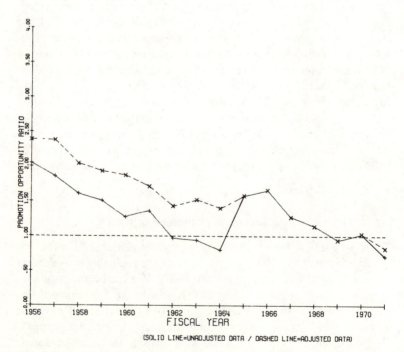

(SOLID LINE=UNADJUSTED DATA / DASHED LINE=ADJUSTED DATA)

Fig. 4. Naval aviators' promotion opportunity ratios, data transformation

Recall that, between FY 1965 and FY 1970, selections from above, within, and below the zone were reported, but that eligibles were reported only for above and within the zone. Total selections were computed as a percentage of total eligibles reported for each of the six years. The result was a range of percentages from approximately 10 to 20 percent. For each of the years from FY 1956 to FY 1964, selections as a percentage of eligibles were calculated on a cumulative year-group basis, starting with the most senior year-group. The subset of year-groups which fell within the range of values based on the FY 1965 to FY 1970 data was stipulated to be comparable to data from the later period, and PORs were calculated on the basis of the subset. A comparison of the unadjusted and transformed data yields an $r = 0.95$ ($p = .05$). An application of the transformation criterion to the FY 1971 data yields a $POR = 0.82$. The actual value of the POR for FY 1971 is 0.71.

Unadjusted and transformed data are shown in figure 4.

8

Conclusion

Like many public sector problems, national security issues are innocent of prominent solutions. Perhaps more than most such problems, national security issues are characterized by passionate commitments to particular stands, often intensified by a sense of selflessness and sacrifice among their official proponents. These features combine to produce policy debates in which reasonable, intelligent, and dedicated participants strongly disagree about what to do but are unanimous in their belief that it is critically important to choose the right course. Questions of national security, in brief, typically have no clear answers *and* zealous advocates of incompatible alternatives. The result is a situation in which the problems of political responsibility and organizational control are especially acute.

The issue is not simply whether the president can prevail over his uniformed subordinates in the national security bureaucracy. The record shows that the president has the power to translate his intention into official action in virtually any case—including securing the removal of U.S. missiles from Turkey before they become entangled in an international crisis.

The fact is that, although he can get almost anything he wants badly enough, he cannot do everything himself: presidents (and scholars) must confront the inescapable reality that the overwhelming proportion of modern foreign policy—both grand and mundane —is the product of formal organizations. The problems of political responsibility and organizational control grow out of the president's need to look to others to do most of what he wants to get done. He must find ways to increase the chances that foreign policy decisions and actions taken by his subordinates converge with and support his policy preferences. Students of international relations must analyze these efforts and understand their consequences.

As Neustadt (1960) showed nearly two decades ago, the power to issue orders is not enough. Although the president has a monopoly of formal authority within the executive branch, it has never proved sufficient. The record of interactions between postwar administrations and the military services provides recurring demonstrations that subordinate compliance cannot be commanded. As leaders in every large organization inevitably discover, even unlimited formal authority cannot eliminate the intrinsic problems of organizational control.

These problems have at least two sources. First, the inescapable delegation of tasks inevitably diffuses influence and diminishes control: the behavior of bureaucratic subordinates cannot be completely directed. As we have seen, a monopoly of formal authority does not constitute a monopoly of bargaining advantages: the simple hierarchy of formal authority within the executive branch obscures the messy reality of hierarchical bargaining. As a result, the president must nudge, entice, and negotiate with his uniformed subordinates as well as seek to command their obedience.

Second, there is no single policy process whose outputs define national security decisions and actions. Instead, there are numerous —often informal—decision streams which are only loosely coupled. This analysis has looked at three such decision processes. It has analyzed the consequences of different procedures for distributing the defense budget as well as the bureaucratic implications of the resource allocations which result. It also has considered the impact of changes in official strategic doctrine. Finally, it has examined the behavior of personnel systems which produce senior military officers as well as the results of handpicking uniformed advisers.

As we have seen, decisions and actions taken in any of these arenas can affect the shape and content of national security policy. The decision streams which produce them, however, are not closely coordinated. They instead affect one another as they irregularly bump and collide. As a result, there are many places in "the" national security policy process at which to apply presidential leverage. Conversely, there are diverse arenas whose unexpected interactions produce surprises and which threaten to dissipate presidential energies and resources.

This diagnosis should not be misread. To observe that politically accountable officials must bargain with their uniformed subordinates is to argue neither that the political leadership is unavoidably hostage to the military services nor that outcomes are invulnerable to manipulation. To note that national security decisions and actions are the products of a loosely coupled system is to argue neither that the results are unpredictable nor that strategies for orchestrating the outputs are impossible. Presidents are *constrained* by the limitations of formal organizations and the bureaucratic facts of life; they are not *paralyzed*.

Presidents and their agents possess preponderant bargaining advantages and ordinarily can achieve most of what they explicitly direct. As our examples of civil-military bargains suggest, moreover, the administration often can secure the support or acquiescence of the military services by making no more than modest concessions. Indeed, the situation which McNamara confronted during the middle and late 1960s is noteworthy in part because of the unlikely convergence of factors—some of which (like Vietnam) were beyond the administration's immediate control—which produced united military opposition to the secretary's decisions while increasing his vulnerability.

On the other hand, politically accountable officials hardly are invincible nor are their bargaining resources inexhaustible. The experiences of a wartime hero as president, and of a brilliant and aggressive secretary of defense, illustrate that neither an extraordinary military reputation nor a dynamic role-image is sufficient to ensure congruence between authoritative decisions and ultimate actions. Politically accountable officials, therefore, must be consciously attentive to the dynamics of the organizations on which they rely and sensitive to the incentives and leverage of the subordinates with whom they negotiate.

The bargaining advantages of these officials ultimately derive from their claims to formal authority and the sanctions permitted by that authority. Our analysis, however, suggests ways in which these participants can strengthen their position by "investing" some of their resources in organizational change. This is not an argument for yet another reorganization of the Defense Department: the failure of successive efforts to overcome the services' "parochialism," competition, and inertia is suggestive of the impotence of formal reorganizations which fail to take account of the participants' incentives and the distribution of sanctions.

Organizational strategies should be based on the recognition that bureaucratic structures and processes interact with the participants' incentives to influence their preferences and actions. These formal relationships and procedures help to establish behaviorally defined boundaries which separate communities of interest and generate patterns of cooperation and conflict. They also reflect the distribution of bargaining advantages among the participants.

Our examination of postwar defense politics has shown that, while the military services have important bargaining resources, they are responsive in the literal sense that they react to changes in the incentives which they face. The resulting combination of limited control and literal responsiveness is the organizational paradox which administration officials must engage. They potentially can enhance their bargaining advantages—and therefore their control—by changing bureaucratic relationships and procedures in ways which exploit the services' capacity for responsiveness. Their objective is to use their official positions and other bargaining resources to manipulate the organizational constraints which they face, to modify their subordinates' incentives, and to strengthen the bargaining advantages of their policy allies.

As we have seen, the structures and procedures which generate the annual defense budgets capture much of the debate and struggle over national security decisions and actions: whatever the decision process which produces or changes national security policy, its results usually leave budgetary traces. These budget data can provide the policy-maker—and the analyst—with quantitative measures of performance and outcomes. Conversely, the president can exploit his formal authority over the defense budget process to affect behavior and outcomes in areas not formally linked to resource allocations. This suggests that, within the Department of Defense at least, authority over the budget process can be used to develop and implement a strategy of influence which challenges the organizational paradox.

This book has examined the defense politics of the Eisenhower administration and the Kennedy-Johnson period from a budgetary perspective in order to evaluate their efforts to achieve their policy objectives. Popular descriptions draw a striking contrast between McNamara's tenure as secretary of defense and the national security policy process during the 1950s. They describe a difference not merely in techniques and maneuvers adopted to ameliorate a commonly perceived problem but a contrast in the very purposes and objectives imputed to the different administrations. These divergent expectations make our findings of substantially indistinguishable budgetary outcomes all the more dramatic.

The convergence between the budgetary outcomes of the 1950s and 1960s can be explained in part by the performance of the Eisenhower administration. The analysis indicates that this administration's participation in the formulation of defense policy was both more active and more effective than the conventional wisdom would suggest. Perhaps more important, the unforeseen defects of defense management, and especially the budgeting process, during the 1960s spawned outcomes which fell short of the spokesmen's claims and expectations.

The problems which the Democratic administrations encountered resulted less from their policy purposes than from their bureaucratic practices. Some of the shortcomings were essentially technical or organizational. For example, the FYDP could not be used to produce annual budget estimates. Likewise, the Comptroller's Office in OSD, which reviewed the services' budget estimates, never was reorganized to parallel the program structure of the defense budget. As a result, budget estimates continued to be reviewed—and re-duced—in terms of traditional appropriations categories.

These kinds of problems can be mitigated or remedied. So too can many of the more serious difficulties which resulted from the refusal to acknowledge the fiscal constraints within which PPBS had to operate. McNamara's successors in fact have provided the services with "fiscal guidance" which set "targets" or "ceilings" on their budget estimates.

Even the bureaucratic and political problems which PPBS spawned can be ameliorated. For example, Melvin Laird attempted to increase the military's sense of "due process" by expanding the services' participation in setting defense priorities and asking the JCS to evaluate the risks associated with trying to achieve national security objectives within fiscal guidance. Allocational rivalries can be nurtured by asking the services to identify equal-cost tradeoffs for any programs which exceed their fiscal guidance.

These strategies are only illustrative. The point to be emphasized is that neither McNamara's policy objectives nor PPBS itself led inexorably to the problems he experienced. Indeed, the behavior of McNamara and his colleagues appears paradoxical in retrospect. Their concentration on restructuring the formal budgeting system suggests an appreciation of the opportunities to exploit the resource allocation process as an instrument of policy and as a mechanism of organizational control. The actual operation of PPBS in Mc-Namara's Pentagon, however, suggests an insensitivity to, if not innocence of, the organizational processes which create the gulf be-tween good decisions and subsequent actions: the administration's dependence on the military services for political support and policy implementation often was disregarded; the officers' incentives seem-ingly were ignored; and the military's bargaining advantages were strengthened. The administration then struggled to overwhelm or circumvent the resulting opposition with bargaining resources which its own actions had dissipated. The tenure of Robert McNamara, in brief, does not provide an entirely fair test of the opportunities for aggressive civilian leadership of the national security bureaucracy.

Looking at the defense politics of the 1950s and 1960s from a budgetary perspective, one sees an incomplete picture of a limited topic. This clearly has not been a book about the national security policies of the Eisenhower and Kennedy-Johnson administrations.

It also has not been intended to be a complete history of their respective purposes, skills, and accomplishments. For example, if the Eisenhower administration deserves greater credit for its bureaucratic success than it usually receives, this may be because it succeeded for reasons and in ways which its members neither intended nor understood. Likewise, if the "McNamara Revolution" failed to achieve dramatic improvements in defense management and organizational control, it did leave a legacy of explicit analysis which has continued to shape national security policies and civil-military interactions.

The book has attempted to understand by what means—and with what consequences—different administrations have sought military compliance with their national security policies. Its purpose has been to illuminate the choices available to future policy-makers. It has described some of the opportunities and booby traps which face administration officials as they negotiate with their uniformed subordinates. It has argued for taking a politically instrumental view of issues relating to formal organizational arrangements and for trying to exploit, rather than overcome, the characteristics of the national security bureaucracy. In particular, it has directed attention to the resource allocation process as a way to increase the leverage which politically accountable officials can have on the shape of national security decisions and actions. At the same time, it has implicitly urged policy-makers to pursue only modest bureaucratic objectives and to pursue them with caution and good preparations for failure. Were it not for the record of postwar defense politics, this advice might seem either presumptuous or self-evident.

Notes

Introduction

1. Kissinger's description of his responsibilities early in the Nixon administration (quoted in Destler 1971–72, p. 32) paints the same picture from the perspective of a central participant: "the outsider believes a Presidential order is consistently carried out. Nonsense. I have to spend considerable time seeing that it is carried out and in the spirit the President intended."

2. The need for such policy theories is suggested by Thomas Schelling's analysis (1966) of the changing role of force in relations among nations. He argues that "coercive diplomacy" has displaced "brute force" in international relations and, accordingly, that the coercive component of a nation's influence in the international arena derives from processes of perception and capabilities for persuasion.

Chapter 1

1. See the appendix to this chapter for a discussion of the variables which affect the analytical power of a budgetary perspective.

2. Approximately twenty-five active-duty military officers from the three services and present or former civilian executives in the Department of Defense were interviewed during 1969 and 1970. Most of the officers were serving in the grade of colonel/captain. Several have since been promoted to flag rank. The civilians interviewed had worked or were working in the Office of the Secretary of Defense. The list of respondents was constructed by asking each to suggest colleagues and associates who would be responsive to my questions. The interviews were informal and confidential. The circumstances required that they be conducted in the form of a casual conversation. The respondents were asked the same open-ended questions but were encouraged to pursue particular points beyond the specific scope of the inquiry. The following areas were discussed: (a) the internal structure of the three services with special reference to the identification of major intraservice factions; (b) the distribution of influence among these groups with particular emphasis on resource allocation decisions; (c) the hierarchy of priorities and objectives expressed in terms of budget categories; (d) interservice relations with special attention to the circumstances which promote competition and cooperation; (e) the relationship between the military services and the civilian administration; and (f) the impact of changes in the formal budget procedures on the above. Additional officers were interviewed about topics related to their formal responsibilities, for example, procedures for preparation of budget estimates and rules governing the identification of officers eligible for promotion. These interviews were supplemented by interviews with a similar group of officials conducted by John P. Crecine during 1974. The respondents in no way are representative of any population. The information acquired during the interviews was not intended to permit generalizations regarding the attitudes and opinions of some larger group. Rather, the interviews were designed to illuminate the results of data analysis and to check on information derived from the scholarly literature and journalistic accounts.

3. The importance attached to the secretary's new budgetary authority for efforts to strengthen his position is suggested by the preamble to the 1949 amendments which describes the primary purpose of the legislation as: "An Act to reorganize the fiscal management in the National Security Establishment . . ." (cited in Mosher 1954, p. 41).

4. All budget data, unless otherwise noted, were supplied by the Department of Defense, Office of the Assistant Secretary of Defense (Comptroller).

5. See Crecine (1966) and Stromberg (1970) for more complete descriptions of the stages of the defense budget cycle. During the Eisenhower years, the Bureau of the Budget (BOB) played a separate but relatively minor role in defense budgeting. During the Kennedy-Johnson years, BOB had virtually no independent role in the formulation of the defense budget (Crecine 1969, p. 27.) Consequently, such data as are available from the BOB stage of the budget cycle are not included in the analysis.

6. For the purposes of this research, budget data collected in terms of "output" categories, for example, Strategic Forces and General Purpose Forces, would be much more preferable. However, data have been produced in this format only since FY 1963, and only for a single stage in budgetary process. They cannot be derived from the line-item format since the budget for each program is spread across several line items and each line item contains the budget requests from fragments of several programs. A 1967 memorandum written in the Office of the Secretary of Defense observed: "The operating costs charged to a single program element may be financed from 20 activities of 5 appropriations. The costs reflected under a single budget activity (e.g., pay of officers) may be distributed to 300 program elements." As will be seen below, this complexity produced serious bureaucratic problems.

The line-item format itself has undergone several changes since 1953. John Stromberg (1970) has "reconstructed" the defense budget since FY 1953 into FY 1969 budget categories in order to permit comparisons across time. The present analysis of the budget line items is based on the data generously provided by Stromberg and the Rand Corporation.

7. Individual line items are highly aggregated and each line item conceals considerable detail. Although there are separate line items for "Aircraft Procurement, Air Force," and "Missile Procurement, Air Force" which are useful in distinguishing the flying Air Force from "silo-sitting" Air Force, other lines of division within the service are obscured. For example, appropriations for the procurement of the bomber, fighter, and transport aircraft which are associated with major intra–Air Force factions are combined in a single line item, "Aircraft Procurement, Air Force." Accordingly, it is not possible to directly infer the relative standing of each group from these data.

8. Since FY 1971, however, a substantial proportion of the growth in the defense budget has occurred outside the regular budget process through the use of supplemental requests (Crecine 1975, pp. 82–84).

9. Wildavsky's colleagues analyzed supplementals for a time series of the nondefense budget and found that supplemental budgets were statistically independent of those factors included in their models of basic appropriations (U.S. Congress, Joint Economic Committee 1967, pp. 252–62).

Chapter 2

1. I am indebted to Herbert Kaufman for his helpful suggestions regarding the topic of organizational boundaries. Recent analyses employing the bureaucratic-politics perspective usually do not discuss the rules for organizational disaggregation which they employ nor can the reader easily infer these decision rules from the analysis. See, for example, Halperin (1972a) and Allison (1971, p. 80n).

2. For a brief organizational history of the Department of Defense, see U.S., Blue Ribbon Defense Panel 1970, pp. 10–20. This somewhat critical—and surprisingly candid—study concluded (p. 22) that a merger of the separate services was neither necessary nor desirable.

3. The significance of the military service as the source of positive and negative sanctions is highlighted by the problems encountered in staffing nonservice positions (e.g., Joint Staff, Office of the Secretary of Defense). The conflicting incentives and career risks faced by officers who stray outside the "mainstream" are documented in U.S., Blue Ribbon Defense Panel (1970, especially Appendix D) and Steinhauser (1972).

4. This possibility also has been suggested by Smith (Personal communication, October 26, 1973).

5. The Blue Ribbon Defense Panel (1970, p. 22) asserted that, as a general rule, organizational boundaries become less salient in combat. For a somewhat different view, see Morris J. Blachman (1973, p. 331): "The Air Force had to have the bombing of the North—it was the only real Air Force show in the Vietnam war. The career men around me felt keenly that their service was at a disadvantage in the war's interservice rivalries."

6. It is perhaps symptomatic of the relatively low salience of intra-Army cleavages that, when Army officers are promoted to flag grade, they remove their branch insignia from their uniforms.

7. Even the missile-firing submarine exception is mitigated somewhat by the Navy's policy (adopted from a concern with personnel retention) of rotating officers and men between attack submarines and ballistic missile submarines.

8. See Kanter (1977) for additional data on intra–Air Force cleavages.

9. It it noteworthy that the annual *Register* of Navy officers has omitted information on source of commission since 1968, thus obscuring the virtually complete monopoly on flag grades held by Annapolis graduates.

10. No one has been promoted to the grade of "fleet admiral" or "general of the army"—five-star ranks—since World War II (Segal and Willick 1968, p. 33).

11. This is likely to be a "cohort" effect which will diminish as increasing numbers of Air Force Academy graduates become general officers. See Kanter (1977) and Margiotta (1975).

Chapter 3

1. This does not mean that the Chiefs' formal positions necessarily reflect their true preferences. Although much of the agreement among them may be what Huntington (1961a, p. 159) has called "artificial," other participants are obliged to rely on the official positions taken by the JCS, even if those positions do not accurately reflect the true sentiments of the Chief individually, and even if the other participants suspect that this is the case. See Snyder (1962, pp. 442–43) for a particularly vivid example of "artificial" agreement among the Chiefs about force levels required by the New Look. See Korb (1976) and Appendix A to the *Report* of the U.S. Blue Ribbon Defense Panel (1970) for organizational histories of the JCS.

2. There seems to be no regular procedure for deciding which issues are addressed by the JCS. While some decisions are the result of the JCS routine, most depend on the initiative of the secretary and the willingness of the services to submit issues to the Chiefs. Each seems to have some latitude to select items which will undergo JCS scrutiny. Although it is very likely, there is no assurance that all "important" issues will be placed on the agenda. For example, throughout the "revolt of the admirals" episode, the JCS never was formally asked for a recommendation on the flush-deck carrier (Hammond 1963).

3. There is surprisingly little systematic analysis to support (or challenge) this virtually universal description of the period. One such effort is Charles Longley's content analysis (1969) of statements by senior military officers on civil-military and interservice themes contained in congressional testimony, service journals, and the *New York Times.*

4. The U.S. Blue Ribbon Defense Panel's description of the "flimsy-buff-green" system (1970, pp. 126–28) illustrates how the formal administrative procedures create strong pressures to reach interservice agreement.

5. Roherty reports (1970, p. 42) that Secretary of Defense Gates adopted the policy of literally joining in JCS deliberations whenever the Chiefs could not reach agreement.

6. Jayne speculates (1969, p. 179) that Air Force Chief of Staff Curtis LeMay opposed the Army ABM plan because Maxwell Taylor had voted against the Air Force's Skybolt missile program: "If this was indeed the case, it would not be the first (nor the last) time that the Chiefs withheld support of other services' programs pending corresponding assistance for their own service."

7. FY 1961 data are based on a very small dollar change ($76 million in a budget of approximately $41 billion) which produces misleadingly large percentage changes and differences. In FY 1961, the budget request for the Army was about 1.4 percent less than FY 1960 appropriations; the Navy figure represented a 6.5 percent increase and the Air Force budget request was about 3 percent less.

8. Even the Army's apparent good fortune in FY 1958 is somewhat misleading and its fate in preceding years is understated. About 40 percent of the increase in the Army's FY 1958 budget is accounted for by the request for procurement. This represented the *first* request for any Army procurement funds in an Eisenhower peacetime budget and a reduction of more than 70 percent in the service's request to the administration for procurement funds (Murphy 1956, p. 251).

9. Eisenhower (1965, p. 252) described this provision as "legalized insubordination" but accepted it as the price of securing the needed reorganization legislation.

10. In part, these tangled relationships are merely the symbol of an underlying reality: changing the law to clarify the lines of formal authority will not, by itself, replace hierarchical bargaining with commands (Ries, 1964). The legal relationships, however, also are part of the reality of bureaucratic bargaining: the multiple lines of formal authority constrain an officer's willingness to accept *any* civilian's claim to unquestioned compliance.

11. Indeed, Eisenhower did not so much push the buildup of strategic airpower on a reluctant Congress as resist congressional pressures for even bigger programs (Jayne 1969, p. 110; and Hammond 1969, pp. 73–74).

12. It should be reemphasized that these line-item aggregations are far from perfect indicators. In the present example, Air Force aircraft procurement would include funds for the procurement of airlift for the Army which, if they could be identified, should be added to the Army military personnel budget in this analysis.

13. In order to highlight congressional actions which are obscured in the budget total by offsetting increases and decreases, congressional action was computed as the sum of the absolute differences across categories.

Chapter 4

1. This list of variables closely resembles Neustadt's (1960) inventory of factors which produce "self-executing orders." See also Halperin (1974, pp. 238–60) for a discussion of the "Limits on Faithful Implementation."

2. See also Rowen (1975) for a discussion of the causes of "The Gap between Policy Enunciation and Operational Behavior."

3. These distinctions, while useful conceptually, would be difficult to operationalize. One special problem derives from the fact that deliberate noncompliance, once detected, is more likely to be punished than either inadvertent or unavoidable noncompliance. It follows that it is in the interest of those who engage in deliberate noncompliance to disguise their misbehavior as unintentional, that is, as either inadvertent or unavoidable. The research problems created by these incentives are obvious. For example, when the U.S. Navy forced Soviet submarines to surface during the Cuban missile crisis, contrary to the president's wishes and intentions, was it an example of the uncalculating implementation of standard operating procedures (inadvertent noncompliance) or a conscious exploitation of an opportunity to build a case for increased resources for antisubmarine warfare forces, notwithstanding the potential consequences for the president's objectives (deliberate noncompliance)? See Allison (1971, p. 138) for an account of this incident.

4. House Appropriations Committee Chairman Mahon explicitly noted that the Joint Chiefs' endorsement was relatively restrained: "Mr. Secretary, of course, it would be almost inevitable that a program of this magnitude would increase our overall combat effectiveness." In reaffirming the adequacy of the proposed budget, McNamara merely referred once again to the Joint Chiefs' endorsement (U.S. Congress, House, 1965 Part III, p. 148).

5. Kennedy's FY 1962 supplemental budget request is a catalogue of bargains struck between the administration and the services (Kaufmann 1964, p. 54). Thus, Herbert York (1970, p. 155) quotes Kennedy's private explanation for continuing the Skybolt program: the administration needed Skybolt to shoot down the B-70. See also Trewhitt (1971, pp. 252–53) on Kennedy's search for JCS support for ratification of the 1963 Limited Test Ban Treaty.

6. The president also confronts a related dilemma. He not only wants military support but also expert advice and real policy alternatives. These twin objectives give rise to the problem of responding to uncongenial recommendations (Halperin 1972b, pp. 310–11, and 320–23).

7. Ironically, persistent efforts by successive postwar administrations to reduce "waste and duplication" in the Pentagon probably have strengthened the services' positions as monopoly suppliers. It is noteworthy that a recent study of the problem (Allison 1975, p. 213) recommends steps to increase competition.

8. Thus, Kennedy initially preferred the "surgical air strike option" to respond to Soviet missiles in Cuba. The operation could only be conducted by the Tactical Air Command (TAC). When TAC refused to give Kennedy adequate assurances that the option was "feasible," he turned his attention to the "quarantine" alternative (Allison 1971, pp. 123–26; and pp. 204–6).

9. It should be emphasized again that much of the business before the JCS is routine. Consequently, it seems reasonable to assume that a substantial—if unknown—proportion of the unanimous recommendations entail no particular significance and demand little additional explanation (Goodpaster 1967, pp. 236–37).

10. The number of rejections probably would have been even higher except that the Air Force chief of staff, Curtis LeMay, frequently joined with McNamara in opposing certain Army and Navy programs and occasionally adopted an even tougher stance than the secretary (for example, fewer aircraft carriers and army divisions than McNamara had recommended). Those services responded by recommending a smaller number of Air Force tactical fighter wings than McNamara proposed.

11. Thus, the JCS statement of "support" for the FY 1966 budget described above was an endorsement of a proposal for a $2.1 billion *reduction* from the preceding year's budget request (as well as $1.1 billion less than Congress had appropriated for FY 1965) which rebuked each of the services on a favorite program.

12. Computed from data presented in Charles L. Schultze, et al. (1971, p. 35).

13. The latter category is more precisely: Research, Development, Testing and Evaluation (RDT & E) which includes funds for advanced development and testing prior to large-scale procurement.

14. There are, of course, several constraints on the administration's ability to distribute resources. We already have mentioned that a substantial proportion of defense spending is fixed in the short term. The role and significance of Congress as a constraint on administration discretion also has been discussed.

Chapter 5

1. Assessing the quality of the Democratic administrations' policy preferences regarding national security is beyond the scope of this analysis.

2. However accurate it may have been as a description of the Eisenhower administration, Hitch's image is a good characterization of the Truman administration. A July 16, 1948 Bureau of the Budget memorandum to the secretary of defense on "Budget Ceiling, Fiscal Year 1950" informed him that: "The President has determined . . . that the authority for new obligations for national defense . . . for fiscal year 1950 shall be limited to $15,000,000,000. . . . [T]his ceiling is presented with a minimum of itemization so that you may have the widest practicable latitude for the formulation of a balanced military program."

3. The same distinction was reiterated (1971, p. 8) in Enthoven and Smith's review of McNamara's tenure: "At issue was not the men [who served prior to 1961], many of whom were exceptionally able and made lasting contributions to the Defense Department; it was the philosophy, structure, and techniques of the Department's management system."

4. It is useful to distinguish among three conceptually distinct components of PPBS because each affected the secretary's influence differently (Schlesinger 1968, pp. 2–5). First, the budget *format* was changed from input categories to output categories: programs and program elements replaced appropriations as the relevant budgetary divisions in the Pentagon. PPBS spokesmen (e.g., Enthoven and Smith 1971, p. 39) argued that this program perspective enhanced their ability to make rational and efficient resource allocation decisions, especially those involving interservice comparisons. Second, an *analytical capability* was developed, primarily in the Office of Systems Analysis, in order to assist the decision-makers in making choices among the alternatives highlighted by the new budget format. Third, a *mechanism for monitoring compliance* by the services with the secretary's resource allocation decisions was devised: the complete list of officially approved defense programs and estimated costs projected for five years were codified in the Five-Year Defense Program (FYDP). It should be emphasized that any one of the three components of PPBS may exist in the absence of the others. Program budgeting does not require systems analysis, nor are administrative mechanisms for monitoring compliance particularly characteristic of PPBS.

5. In certain years, the services submitted two budget estimates: one, the "basic" budget, was restricted to requests for programs explicitly approved by the secretary; the second, the "addendum" budget, included budget requests for programs which, for a variety of reasons, the secretary had not formally approved.

6. Judging whether there were in fact ceilings on the defense budget during the 1950s requires the drawing of subtle, and perhaps meaningless distinctions. Bureau of the Budget memoranda (e.g., July 19, 1956) indicate that it did not impose "ceilings" on the FY 1957 and FY 1958 defense budgets. It did plan "targets" for DOD in FY 1957. The Bureau reported to the president (Bureau of the Budget, January 19, 1956), however, that "the figures were not accepted" by the secretary of defense and complained this refusal led the services to produce "detailed budget requests which build up to excessive totals way beyond that which is finally allowed." An October 3, 1957, BOB memorandum acknowledged the secretary of defense's subsequent cooperation but noted the services' noncompliance: "Although Secretary [of Defense] Wilson directed that budgets be submitted to his office by October 1 within limits of $38.0 billion expenditure, the services have not complied with this directive." In 1959, the civilian secretaries of the services agreed that: "The basic budget submissions of the military departments [for FY 1961], in terms of new obligational authority, would be within an amount equal to the 1960 effective NOA [New Obligational Authority]." Nevertheless, the Eisenhower administration reduced the services' budget estimates for FY 1961 by 8 percent before sending its budget to Congress.

7. This choice is said to be based—or rationalized—on the congenial assumption that any budget stringency will be temporary and that any deficit in readiness can be quickly remedied when the budget pressures are relaxed. For a similar view, see Enthoven and Smith (1971, p. 336). For a somewhat different view, based on the imputation of economic rationality to the participants, see Stromberg (1970, p. 146).

8. Procurement and O & M become leading candidates for budget reductions somewhat by default. The RDT & E account, typically, is only 10 or 12 percent of the total. Accordingly, even very large reductions in this category would produce only modest changes in the total budget. The Military Personnel account is largely fixed, being a function of the number of men in uniform times their respective pay rates. Since the size of the force in part is determined outside the budget context, and since the pay rates are legislated separately, there is little room for reduction in the personnel budget during budget review.

9. This line item does not distinguish among whatever priorities exist among different kinds of aircraft (e.g., bombers, fighters, transport). The analysis therefore includes the substantial cuts in the procurement of transport aircraft—widely regarded as a low Air Force priority—which occurred during the 1950s.

10. The dominance of aviators within the Navy is documented in Chapter 7. Unfortunately, Navy aircraft procurement does not appear as a separate line item. A significant number of Navy missiles are associated with the naval air mission, either as air-launched missiles or ship-to-air fleet defense missiles. An obvious exception are the Polaris/Poseidon missiles whose procurement costs also are included in this line item. However, subtracting these costs (based on data given in Sapolsky 1972, p. 171) produced no substantial changes.

11. This is not to deny that attention to fiscal constraints were a central feature of the New Look. Eisenhower himself argued (1963, p. 446): "national security could not be measured in terms of military strength alone. The relationship . . . between military and economic strength is intimate and indivisible."

12. In an ironic foretaste of the congressional criticism of McNamara's civilian "whiz kids" in the 1960s, Defense Appropriations Subcommittee

Chairman George Mahon attacked Eisenhower's reductions in the FY 1954 Air Force budget, saying, "civilians in the Pentagon with no military experience are thwarting the will of Congress" (quoted in Congressional Quarterly 1953, p. 138). Contrary to popular impression, what distinguished the Eisenhower airpower programs from those of his predecessor was not his strong emphasis on offensive strategic airpower but rather his consistent support for air *defense* programs. According to George Quester (1970, p. 103): "The expansion of air defenses constituted the Eisenhower administration's largest and most voluntary augmentation of defense expenditures." In fact, Eisenhower postponed large-scale procurement of the B-52 strategic aircraft in order to make additional funds available for air defense.

13. Eisenhower (1963, p. 452) leaves little doubt that his defense preferences were communicated to the military services. Taylor's observations are particularly significant precisely because of his intense opposition to the New Look strategy. It is implausible that he would have objected so strongly to official doctrine, or devoted so much attention to what he believed to be the flaws in Eisenhower's budget system, if Eisenhower in fact granted to the services substantial spending autonomy within the ceiling he imposed.

14. Although he derived it from a somewhat different analysis, Stromberg (1970) reached a similar conclusion concerning the absence of striking differences in the budgets of the two time periods.

15. The arbitrariness in the allocation of costs among program elements is revealed by an example related by a former OSD official: a fixed percentage of operating overhead was charged to a particular anti-submarine warfare program element. Since the overhead costs were not directly related to the number of aircraft in operation, the overhead charged to this program element did not change as the aircraft became obsolescent and were phased out. This finally resulted in a situation in which *none* of these aircraft remained in inventory but several million dollars were charged to their operation.

16. The Army colonel offered a complementary explanation for the decline in requests for new programs, namely, they were useless: it was futile to spend time preparing requests for FYDP changes which OSD could be expected to reject routinely. His description supports Stromberg's finding (1970, p. 124) that the services discovered "that the 'pricing out' procedure was sufficiently flexible that [they] . . . could come in with very high initial estimates even while adhering to the basic plan." See also Murdock (1971, p. 15) for a similar response by the Air Force in 1964.

17. Enthoven and Smith confessed (1971, p. 289), "Often it is difficult for even DOD management, much less the Congress and the public, to recognize the difference [between "paper" shortages and real shortages]."

18. If resources literally were unconstrained, of course, the "cost" side of the frequently controversial cost-effectiveness calculations would be zero, and such considerations would have been unnecessary. In this fundamental sense, there must have been some limit on the defense budget in the 1960s. The concept relating marginal costs to marginal increments in "national security" became obscured in public (and private) justifications which contrasted budget-making in McNamara's Pentagon with the practices of his predecessors. Instead, popular images of the defense budget process during the two time periods painted a picture of the 1950s in which a defense budget was predetermined and then was spent to buy "national security" compared to the 1960s in which the annual defense budget was simply the sum of the costs of programs required for "national security." I am indebted to Arnold Kuzmack for suggesting this conceptualization of alternative budget-making processes.

For the record, the Eisenhower administration also publicly denied that it imposed budget ceilings on the Pentagon. In 1956, Secretary of Defense Wilson testified: "The President never said to me 'There is a certain [budget] figure that the Defense Department has to get down to.' . . . I can say that nothing was deleted [from the defense budget request] from pressure to balance the budget" (Quoted in Congressional Quarterly 1956, p. 611).

19. This problem was noted by the Bureau of the Budget as early as 1962. (U.S. Bureau of the Budget, 1962).

20. This description bears a close—and ironic—resemblance to Hammond's account (1961, p. 307) of the Eisenhower administration. Hammond observed (with some distress) that the official planning documents prepared by the services ordinarily were not completed in time for the annual budget decisions which, in theory, they were to inform: "The fiscal decisions are made first, and being made first, they are determinative of strategy and other military policy."

Chapter 6

1. Across-time comparisons of OSD budget data should be made with caution. Certain joint agencies were created during the late 1950s and early 1960s (Defense Communications Agency, Defense Supply Agency, Defense Intelligence Agency) and were funded as part of the OSD budget. Prior to the creation of these agencies, funding of their activities was divided between OSD and the services.

2. Calculated from data reported in U.S., Department of Defense, Directorate for Statistical Services, *Selected Manpower Statistics*, April 15, 1969, p. 24. This growth cannot be attributed either to an overall increase in defense personnel or to increased manpower demands during the Vietnam War. The number of active-duty commissioned officers was approximately constant or declining throughout the period: the size of the FY 1954 officer corps was not reached again until FY 1968. Moreover, the annual rate of growth of OSD during the 1960s was about the same during the Vietnam War (6.34 percent) as before (6.07 percent).

3. The impact of formal policy statements on behavior is suggested by the intensity of the struggle which attends their formulation. Snyder (1962, pp. 437–38) describes the fight over the language in the 1953 Basic National Security Paper regarding the description of strategic nuclear power as "the" deterrent rather than "a major" deterrent. For a similar episode, see Taylor's account (1960, pp. 38–39) of the conflict over the definition of "general war."

4. For another view of the bureaucratic consequences of strategic doctrine, see Allison (1975, chap. 3). As Allison notes (p. 47) "Choice of an official strategic objective with reference not only to a preferred objective, but also to affecting service bargaining leverage is a subtle and little-explored issue."

5. McNamara's deep involvement in the conduct of the "quarantine" during the Cuban missile crisis provides a good counterexample.

6. Such doubts frequently are expressed in the context or discussions of military "professionalism." The military's claims to unique expertise were increasingly defended in print in response to apparent challenges posed by the McNamara administration. See Ginsburgh (1964) and Thayer (1971). See also Korb (1976, pp. 119–20).

7. Eisenhower did occasionally exploit his professional credentials. See Snyder (1962, p. 448) on the pressures applied to Army Chief of Staff Ridgway to endorse the administration's programs. It may be that Eisenhower's claims to military expertise were sufficiently self-evident as to not require explicit reference (Legere and Davis 1969a). In particular, he had been General of the *Army,* precisely the service most disadvantaged by his strategic policies.

8. Ridgway understood these consequences. He objected that "for the Chiefs to make such an assessment [of economic feasibility and impact] . . . would be dangerous because it would deprive the civilian leadership of undiluted, objective professional judgment on the military factors" (quoted in Snyder 1962, p. 432).

9. The civilians repeatedly demonstrated that, if the services were unable or unwilling to perform satisfactory analyses, the Office of Systems Analysis would fill the vacuum (Hitch 1965, p. 57; Niskanen 1969, p. 21). By the mid-1960s, counteradvocacy based on competing (and self-serving) analyses had replaced the one-sided advocacy based on Office of Systems Analysis studies. For example, the Air Force produced a study which "demonstrated" that manned bombers were more cost-effective than missiles for the administration's policy of damage limitation. The officer who described this study added that the analysis had been performed exclusively by military officers with no assistance from civilians in OSD. Indeed, he implied that the civilians would not have been able to conduct such a study (confidential interview).

10. Somewhat surprisingly, the quoted phrase is from Enthoven and Smith (1971, p. 327). Their retrospective evaluation of McNamara's tenure hints at an awareness of some of the unanticipated consequences of the budgeting system over which they presided. See especially Chapter 9: "Unfinished Business, 1969."

11. It should be noted that McNamara often sought to characterize his rejections of the Chiefs' positions as reflecting disagreements about technical details (pace of modernization, timing of phase-in or phase-out of weapons systems, when to move from R & D to procurement) rather than about the military value of the programs. On the other hand, he explained to the president that he was able to reduce the services' budget estimates by eliminating "all *non-essential, marginal,* and postponable expenditures" (McNamara 1964, emphasis added).

12. This assumes that the participants do not challenge the total budget ceiling but rather direct their attention to increasing their respective proportions. Eisenhower reported (1971, p. 23) that this was the case during the 1950s: "The JCS constantly would tell me that the sums placed before the Congress were quite ample. But each [Chief] always said that he needed a bit more of the pie."

13. Air Force Chief of Staff Curtis LeMay testified (U.S. Congress, House, 1964, Part IV, p. 511): "I am sure if we [in the military services] had [looked at the total cost of the proposals] we would have cut that total down because it was an unreasonable budget to ask for. We would have established priorities and cut some." The services' incentives to ask for more of everything also concentrated the political *responsibility* for decisions on OSD: if inadequacies or failures in defense policy were subsequently charged by external critics, the services were officially on record with their recommendations and warnings of dire consequences.

14. Cf. Selznick (1949, p. 259) on the distinction between power and "the burdens of power."

15. Such duplication was proposed by Maxwell Taylor precisely as a procedure to reduce interservice rivalries (Taylor 1960, p. 167). Functional rivalries frequently are stimulated by technological development—particularly new weapons capabilities—which disrupt the existing division of labor. The 1960s saw far fewer destabilizing developments than the preceding period (atomic weapons, long-range aircraft, missiles, etc.). Ironically, McNamara's reluctance to fund vaguely defined research and development projects directed at technological progress per se may have contributed to the dimunition of functional rivalries (cf. Roherty 1970, pp. 106–13).

Chapter 7

1. There also is some evidence to suggest that Eisenhower's choices for the Joint Chiefs were responsive to pressures from the Republican-controlled Congress (or the Republican party). Specifically, Eisenhower consulted with party leaders concerning his candidates and Robert Taft gave his approval before they were publicly announced. See, Fergus (1968) and Snyder (1962).

2. As noted above, although the temptation to indulge in this tactic is nearly irresistible, its use endangers the image of military professionalism which the administration wishes to exploit—and struggles to harness. Maxwell Taylor's criticism of Eisenhower echoes Robert Taft's complaint about Truman. In Taylor's view (1960, p. 20), the installation of a new JCS in the opening months of the new administration "suggested that the Joint Chiefs belonged to the administration in power and were expected to be the spokesmen for its military policy. This concept of role was quite different from that previously accepted." Cf. Eisenhower (1963, p. 448).

3. Glenn Snyder reports (1962, p. 412) that Radford initially was chosen by Secretary of Defense Wilson.

4. Snyder (1962) details the Eisenhower administration's tortured search for the Chiefs' endorsement of the New Look and the budgets which flowed from the doctrine.

5. Korb (1970, p. 10) attributes this view to Admirals McDonald and Anderson.

6. As a corollary, almost any administration proposal can trace its heritage to an earlier recommendation by a military service. For example, many of McNamara's proposals found immediate support—and historical precedent—among parts of the military services. The Army had argued for a doctrine of "flexible response" throughout the 1950s as a counter to the New Look strategy which threatened its vitality (Taylor 1960). McNamara's proposal for a counterforce strategy, outlined in his famous 1962 Ann Arbor speech, had been recommended earlier by the Air Force as a continuing justification for the manned bomber (Kaufmann 1964). Even program budgeting had been advocated by the Army and Navy during the 1950s in the hope of capturing some of the Air Force's share of the defense budget (Grosse and Proschan 1967). As Henry Kissinger once remarked (1973, p. 89): "Most ideas that masquerade as new ideas in Washington have been around for quite a long time."

7. This description, of course, closely resembles Neustadt's analysis (1960, p. 34): "The essence of a President's persuasive task is . . . to convince men [on whom he depends] that what the White House wants of them is what they ought to do for their own sake and on their own authority."

8. See Halperin (1974, pp. 23–35) for his characterization of the organizational "essence" of each of the military services.

9. Vincent Davis's analysis of the postwar Navy (1966) highlights the importance which the participants themselves attach to dominating the senior ranks in the service. He argues that the naval aviators adopted a deliberate and calculated strategy designed to give them control of the flag grades. For example, the aviators lobbied for legislation to lower the statutory age of retirement for flag officers and to increase the authorized number of admirals from 91 to 118. Their twin objectives were to force the retirement of their intraservice opponents—the battleship admirals—and to create new positions at flag grade into which the aviators could be promoted.

10. Charles Perrow (1961, pp. 855–56) draws a useful distinction between an organization's "official" goals and its "operative" goals. He defines official goals as "the general purposes of the organization as put forth in the charter, annual reports, public statements by key executives and other authoritative pronouncements." By contrast, "Operative goals designate the ends sought through the actual operating policies of the organization; they tell us what the organization is actually trying to do, regardless of what the official goals say are the aims."

11. These data were furnished by the Navy Department and by the Department of the Air Force. Since promotions can be made only as vacancies actually occur, these data report officers *selected* for promotion. The analysis is confined to unrestricted line officers in the Navy and to "line" officers in the Air Force. These promotion categories, which account for about 90 percent of the officers in each service, include all of the traditional combat functions and represent the range of policy alternatives generated by the services' roles and missions. The remaining 10 percent of officers are members of noncombat technical specialties, for

example, doctors and chaplains, and do not compete with the line officers for promotion. The omission of data on Army promotions is symptomatic of the differences in the internal structure of the services described in Chapter 2. Recall that the Army was characterized by considerable cross-cutting cleavages. Accordingly, there are less likely to be distinctive intraservice groups and organizationally based policy perspectives. As a corollary, the Army may be less susceptible to influence by manipulation of its organizational environment than either the Navy or the Air Force.

12. As Korb shows (1976, pp. 32–33), these attempts have not been notably successful.

13. During the period analyzed, there were no naval officers of one-star rank (commodores). Navy captains were promoted directly to two-star rank, becoming "lower-half" rear admirals with the same perquisites and status as brigadier generals.

14. See MacCloskey (1967) for a description of these commands. The Air Force data do not distinguish between rated and nonrated officers within commands.

15. See Martin (1969) for a description of the Navy promotion system which has general applicability to the other services.

16. There also is a procedure known as "deep selection" from "below the zone" in the Navy, and from the equivalent "secondary zone" in the Air Force. Officers who are deep selected are those who do not have sufficient seniority to be included within the zone but whose performance has been judged sufficiently outstanding to warrant early selection (Margiotta 1975, pp. 5, 17). The composition of such deep selections may be thought of as a "leading indicator" of trends in promotion patterns: specially advantaged intraservice groups should enjoy even greater benefits among the group of deep-selected officers. Accordingly, the limited data on deep selections are analyzed below for suggestive insights.

17. The extent and the consequences of the board members' discretion appear to be widely understood within the services. This recognition is perhaps best symbolized by the considerable efforts expended to achieve "balanced" selection boards which include representatives from each of the major—but informal—intraservice factions. Even the format of data belies the services' official position that internal cleavages are irrelevant to promotion decisions. For example, the Air Force compiles its promotion statistics (for internal dissemination) in lists which are *rank-ordered* on the basis of percentage of each category (faction) selected for promotion.

18. Promotion opportunity ratios for the period FY 1956 to FY 1964 are based on transformed data. See the appendix to this chapter for a discussion of the transformation procedures.

19. Although the majority of Air Force officers are nonrated, this is due to a preponderance of nonrated personnel in the junior grades. The proportion of officers of a given rank who are rated increases steadily with grade. The majority of Air Force majors are qualified for flying duties. Approximately 90 percent of the general officers are rated.

20. Promotion opportunity ratios for the especially outstanding officers selected from the secondary zone—our "leading indicator"—display the same trend in exaggerated terms. These secondary zone PORs tended to decline both sooner and faster than the overall SAC promotion opportunity ratios. By the late 1960s, the probability of a SAC lieutenant colonel being selected for unusually early promotion was substantially less than that for officers assigned to the "limited war command." If secondary zone selections are a perhaps self-fulfilling prophecy of the Air Force's view of its future and of which officers will make the greatest contribution, the role of SAC in shaping and controlling that future during the 1960s was limited and declining. It should be noted, however, that the number of selections from the secondary zone is quite small. As a result, PORs based on secondary zone selections are volatile and should be interpreted with caution.

21. The reconstruction of the Eisenhower budgets into a program budget format was undertaken by the Office of Management and Budget and was provided to the author by John P. Crecine.

22. The truncated time-series, missing data, and time lags combine to limit the number of pairs of data points used in this calculation to twelve. The results, therefore, should be interpreted with caution.

23. It should be noted that this is a fairly undemanding requirement for a budgeting mechanism to meet: the analysis indicates that the services were about as responsive during the Eisenhower administration—with its somewhat more primitive formal budgeting procedures—as during McNamara's tenure.

References

Allison, Graham T. 1971. *Essence of decision.* Boston: Little, Brown.
————. **1975.** Overview of findings and recommendations from defense and arms control cases. In *U.S. commission on the organization of the government for the conduct of foreign policy. Appendix K: Adequacy of current organization: Defense and arms control.* Washington: Government Printing Office.
Allison, Graham T., and Szanton, Peter. 1976. *Remaking foreign policy.* New York: Basic Books.
Arkes, Hadley. 1972. *Bureaucracy, the Marshall Plan, and the national interest.* Princeton: Princeton University Press.
Blachman, Morris J. 1973. The stupidity of intelligence. In *Readings in American foreign policy,* ed. Morton H. Halperin and Arnold Kanter. Boston: Little, Brown.
Chu, David S. C., and White, John P. 1975. Developing the military executive. In *U.S. commission on the organization of the government for the conduct of foreign policy. Appendix P: Personnel for foreign affairs.* Washington: Government Printing Office.
Congressional Quarterly. 1953. *Almanac 9.*
————. **1956.** *Almanac 12.*
Crecine, John P. 1969. *Defense budgeting.* Discussion Paper no. 6. Ann Arbor: University of Michigan Institute of Public Policy Studies.
————. **1975.** Making defense budgets. In *U.S. commission on the organization of the government for the conduct of foreign policy. Appendix K: Adequacy of current organization: Defense and arms control.* Washington: Government Printing Office.
Cronin, Thomas E. 1970. 'Everybody believes in democracy until he gets to the White House . . .'. *Law and contemporary problems* 35: 573–625.
Cyert, Richard M., and March, James G. 1963. *A behavioral theory of the firm.* Englewood Cliffs, N.J.: Prentice-Hall.
Davis, Vincent. 1966. *Postwar defense policy and the U.S. Navy, 1943–1946.* Chapel Hill: University of North Carolina Press.
Deagle, Edwin A. 1975. NSSM1. In *U.S. commission on the organization of the government for the conduct of foreign policy, Appendix K: Adequacy of current organization: Defense and arms control.* Washington: Government Printing Office.
Destler, I. M. 1971–72. Can one man do? *Foreign Policy,* no. 5:28–40.
————. **1972.** *Presidents, bureaucrats, and foreign policy.* Princeton: Princeton University Press.
Downs, Anthony. 1967. *Inside bureaucracy.* Boston: Little, Brown.
Dulles, John Foster. 1957. Challenge and response in United States policy. *Foreign Affairs* 36:25–43.
Eisenhower, Dwight D. 1963. *Mandate for change: 1953–1956.* Garden City, N.Y.: Doubleday.

————. 1965. *Waging peace: 1956–1961*. Garden City, N.Y.: Doubleday.

————. 1967. The central role of the president in the conduct of security affairs. In *Issues of national security in the 1970s*, ed. Amos A. Jordan, Jr. New York: Praeger.

————. 1971. Eisenhower at the Naval War College. *U.S. Naval Institute Proceedings* 97:18–24.

Enthoven, Alain C., and Smith, K. Wayne. 1971. *How much is enough?* New York: Harper and Row.

Feld, Maury D. 1967. Military self-image in a technological environment. In *The new military*, ed. Morris Janowitz. New York: Wiley Science Editions.

Fergus, Martin C. 1968. The massive retaliation doctrine. *Public Policy* 17:231–57.

Frank, Forrest B. 1975. CBW. In *U.S. commission on the organization of the government for the conduct of foreign policy. Appendix K: Adequacy of current organization: Defense and arms control.* Washington: Government Printing Office.

Gallucci, Robert L. 1975. Fighting in South Vietnam. In *U.S. commission on the organization of the government for the conduct of foreign policy. Appendix K: Adequacy of current organization: Defense and arms control.* Washington: Government Printing Office.

Ginsburgh, Robert N. 1964. The challenge to military professionalism. *Foreign Affairs* 42:255–68.

Goodpaster, Andrew J. 1967. The role of the Joint Chiefs of Staff in the national security structure. In *Issues of national security in the 1970s*, ed. Amos A. Jordan, Jr. New York: Praeger.

Greenberg, George D. 1972. Governing HEW. Ph.D. dissertation, Harvard University.

Grosse, Robert N., and Proschan, Arnold. 1967. The annual cycle: Planning-Programming-Budgeting. In *Defense management*, ed. Stephen Enke. Englewood Cliffs, N.J.: Prentice-Hall.

Halperin, Morton H. 1971. Why bureaucrats play games. *Foreign Policy*, no. 2:70–90.

————. 1972a. The decision to deploy the ABM: Bureaucratic and domestic politics in the Johnson Administration. *World Politics* 25:62–95.

————. 1972b. The President and the military. *Foreign Affairs* 50:310–24.

————. 1974. *Bureaucratic politics and foreign policy.* Washington: Brookings Institution.

Hammond, Paul Y. 1961. *Organizing for defense.* Princeton: Princeton University Press, 1961.

————. 1963. Super carriers and B-36 bombers. In *American civil-military decisions*, ed. Harold Stein. University, Ala: University of Alabama Press for the Twentieth Century Fund.

————. 1968. A functional analysis of Defense Department decision-making in the McNamara Administration. *American Political Science Review* 62:57–69.

————. 1969. *The cold war years.* New York: Harcourt, Brace, and World.

References

Harrelson, Joseph S., Jr. 1968. The Joint Chiefs of Staff and national security. Ph.D. dissertation, American University.
Henry, John B., II. 1971. February, 1968. *Foreign Policy*, no. 4:3–33.
Hirschman, Albert O. 1970. *Exit, voice, and loyalty.* Cambridge: Harvard University Press.
Hitch, Charles J. 1965. *Decision-Making for defense.* Berkeley: University of California Press.
Hitch, Charles J., and McKean, Roland N. 1966. *The economics of defense in the nuclear age.* New York: Atheneum.
Holden, Matthew, Jr. 1966. Imperialism in bureaucracy. *American Political Science Review* 60:943–51.
Hoopes, Townsend, 1969. The fight for the President's mind. *Atlantic Monthly*, October, pp. 97–114.
Hunter, Robert E. 1973. The politics of defense, 1963. In *Readings in American foreign policy*, ed. Morton H. Halperin and Arnold Kanter. Boston: Little, Brown.
Huntington, Samuel P. 1961a. *The common defense.* New York: Columbia University Press.
————. **1961b.** Interservice competition and the political roles of the armed services. *American Political Science Review* 55:40–52.
Jackson, Henry M., ed. 1965. *The National Security Council.* New York: Praeger.
Jayne, Edward R., II. 1969. The ABM debate. Ph.D. dissertation, Massachusetts Institute of Technology.
Jones, William M. 1973. On decisionmaking in large organizations. In *Readings in American foreign policy*, ed. Morton H. Halperin and Arnold Kanter. Boston: Little, Brown.
Kanter, Arnold. 1972. Congress and the defense budget: 1960–1970. *American Political Science Review* 66:129–43.
————. **1977.** The career patterns of Air Force generals. *American Journal of Political Science* 22:353–79.
Kanter, Arnold, and Thorson, Stuart J. 1972. The weapons procurement process: Choosing among competing theories. *Public Policy* 20:479–524.
Kaufman, Herbert. 1960. *The forest ranger.* Baltimore: Johns Hopkins Press for Resources for the Future.
————. **1971.** *The limits of organizational change.* University, Ala: University of Alabama Press.
————. **1973.** *Administrative feedback.* Washington: Brookings Institution.
Kaufmann, William W. 1964. *The McNamara strategy.* New York: Harper and Row.
Kennedy, Robert F. 1969. *Thirteen Days.* New York: New American Library, Signet Books.
Kissinger, Henry A. 1973. Bureaucracy and policymaking: The effect of insiders and outsiders on the policy process. In *Readings in American foreign policy*, ed. Morton H. Halperin and Arnold Kanter. Boston: Little, Brown.
Korb, Lawrence J. 1970. Budget strategies of the Joint Chiefs of Staff, (Fiscal) 1965–1968. Paper presented at the 1970 annual meeting of the American Political Science Association. Los Angeles, Calif.

————. **1976.** *The Joint Chiefs of Staff.* Bloomington: Indiana University Press.

Landsberger, Henry A. 1961. The horizontal dimension in bureaucracy. *Administrative Science Quarterly* 6:299–332.

Lang, Kurt. 1967. Technology and career management in the military establishment. In *The New Military*, ed. Morris Janowitz, New York: Wiley Science Editions.

Legere, Laurence J., and Davis, Vincent. 1969a. A decade of change in the Department of Defense. In *The president and the management of national security*, ed. Keith C. Clark and Laurence J. Legere. New York: Praeger.

————. **1969b.** Prospects and possibilities for the Department of Defense. In *The president and the management of national security*, ed. Keith C. Clark and Laurence J. Legere. New York: Praeger.

Lindblom, Charles E. 1955. *Bargaining: The hidden hand in government.* Santa Monica, Calif.: Rand.

————. **1968.** *The policy-making process.* Englewood Cliffs, N.J.: Prentice-Hall.

Longley, Charles H. 1969. Politics in the Pentagon. Ph.D. dissertation, University of North Carolina.

Lucas, William A., and Dawson, Raymond H. 1974. *The organizational politics of Defense.* Occasional paper no. 2. Pittsburgh: International Studies Association.

MacCloskey, Monro. 1967. *The United States Air Force.* New York: Praeger.

McKean, Roland N., and Anshen, Melvin. 1967. Limitations, risks, and problems. In *Planning, programming, budgeting*, ed. Fremont J. Lyden and Ernest G. Miller. Chicago: Markham.

McNamara, Robert S. 1961. Memorandum for the President on Recommended Department of Defense FY '63 Budget, and 1963–1967 Program. October 6, 1961.

————. **1963.** Memorandum for the President on Could the Defense Department budget be cut to $43 billion without weakening the security of the United States? April 17, 1963.

————. **1964.** Memorandum for the President on Defense Department budget for 1966. December 8, 1964.

————. **1968.** *Essence of security.* New York: Harper and Row.

March, James G. 1962. The business firm as a political coalition. *Journal of Politics* 24:662–78.

March, James G., and Simon, Herbert A. 1958. *Organizations.* New York: Wiley.

Margiotta, Franklin D. 1975. Making it in the Air Force: Officer perceptions of career progression. Paper presented at the 1975 biennial meeting of the Inter-University Seminar on Armed Forces and Society, Chicago, Illinois.

Marshall, A. W. 1966. *Problems of estimating military power.* Santa Monica, Calif.: Rand.

Martin, James K. 1969. Officer promotion planning. *Naval War College Review* 22:68–74.

Merewitz, Leonard, and Sosnick, Stephen H. 1971. *The budget's new clothes.* Chicago: Markham.

Mosher, Frederick C. 1954. *Program budgeting.* Chicago: Public Administration Service.

Murdock, Clark A. 1971. Impact of McNamara's analytic innovations on civil-military relations. Paper presented at the 1971 annual meeting of the International Studies Association.

Murphy, Charles J. V. 1956. Eisenhower's most critical defense budget. *Fortune,* December, p. 112.

Neustadt, Richard E. 1960. *Presidential politics.* New York: Wiley.

————. **1970.** *Alliance politics.* New York: Columbia University Press.

————. **1973.** White House and Whitehall. In *Readings in American foreign policy,* ed. Morton H. Halperin and Arnold Kanter. Boston: Little, Brown.

Niskanen, William A. 1967. The defense resource allocation process. In *Defense management,* ed. Stephen Enke. Englewood Cliffs, N.J.: Prentice-Hall.

————. **1969.** Defense management after McNamara. *Armed Forces Journal,* February, pp. 17–21.

Peabody, Robert L. 1962. Perceptions of organizational authority. *Administrative Science Quarterly* 6:463–82.

Perrow, Charles. 1961. Analysis of goals in complex organizations. *American Sociological Review* 12:854–66.

Ponturo, John. 1969. The president and policy guidance. In *The president and the management of national security,* ed. Keith C. Clark and Laurence J. Legere. New York: Praeger.

Powell, Craig. 1967. Civilian/military rapport reaches a new maturity in the defense area. *Armed Forces Management* 14:47–49.

Quarles, Donald. 1956. How much is enough? *Air Force* 39:51–53.

Quester, George H. 1970. *Nuclear diplomacy.* New York: Dunellen.

Ries, John C. 1964. *The management of defense.* Baltimore: Johns Hopkins Press.

Riordan, Stephen J., Jr. 1958. Budgeting and organization: Their interplay in the Navy Department. M.A. thesis, George Washington University.

Roherty, James M. 1970. *Decisions of Robert S. McNamara.* Coral Gables, Fla.: University of Miami Press.

Rosser, Richard F. 1973. A twentieth-century military force. *Foreign Policy,* no. 12:156–75.

Rowen, Henry S. 1975. Formulating strategic doctrine. In *U.S. commission on the organization of the government for the conduct of foreign policy. Appendix K: Adequacy of current organization: Defense and arms control.* Washington: Government Printing Office.

Sapolsky, Harvey M. 1972. *The Polaris system development.* Cambridge: Harvard University Press.

Schelling, Thomas C. 1966. *Arms and influence.* New Haven: Yale University Press.

————. **1970.** PPBS and foreign affairs. In *Planning-Programming-Budgeting.* U.S. Congress, Senate, Committee on Government Operations, 91st Cong., 2nd sess.

Schick, Allen. 1967. The road to PPB: The stages of budget reform. In *Planning, programming, budgeting,* ed. Fremont J. Lyden and Ernest G. Miller. Chicago: Markham.

Schilling, Warner R. 1962. The politics of national defense: Fiscal 1950. In *Strategy, politics, and defense budgets,* by Warner R. Schilling, Paul Y. Hammond, and Glenn H. Snyder. New York: Columbia University Press.

Schlesinger, James R. 1968. *Defense planning and budgeting.* Santa Monica, Calif.: Rand.

Schultze, Charles L. 1968. *The politics and economics of public spending.* Washington: Brookings Institution.

Schultze, Charles L.; Fried, Edward R.; Rivlin, Alice M.; and Teeters, Nancy H. 1971. *Setting national priorities: The 1972 budget.* Washington: Brookings Institution.

Segal, David R. 1967. Selective promotion in officer cohorts. *Sociological Quarterly* 8:199–206.

Segal, David R., and Willick, Daniel H. 1968. The reinforcement of traditional career patterns in agencies under stress. *Public Administration Review* 28:30–38.

Selznick, Philip. 1949. *TVA and the grass roots.* Berkeley: University of California Press.

Simon, Herbert A.; Smithburg, Donald W.; and Thompson, Victor A. 1970. *Public administration.* New York: Knopf.

Smith, Perry McCoy. 1970. *The Air Force plans for peace, 1943–1945.* Baltimore: Johns Hopkins Press.

Snyder, Glenn H. 1962. The New Look of 1953. In *Strategy, politics, and defense budgets,* by Warner R. Schilling, Paul Y. Hammond, and Glenn H. Snyder. New York: Columbia University Press.

Sorensen, Theodore C. 1966. *Kennedy.* New York: Bantam Books.

Steinhauser, Thomas C. 1972. How to make flag rank . . . don't wander far from home. *Armed Forces Journal,* July 1972, p. 20.

Stromberg, John L. 1970. *The internal mechanisms of the Defense budget process, fiscal 1953–1968.* Santa Monica, Calif.: Rand.

Taylor, Maxwell D. 1960. *The uncertain trumpet.* New York: Harper and Bros.

————. **1963–64.** Military advice: Its use in government. *Vital Speeches* 30:336–39.

Thayer, Frederick C. 1971. Professionalism: The hard choice. *U.S. Naval Institute Proceedings* 97:36–40.

Thompson, Victor A. 1961. *Modern organization.* New York: Knopf.

Trewhitt, Henry L. 1971. *McNamara.* New York: Harper and Row.

U.S. Blue Ribbon Defense Panel. 1970. *Report to the president and the secretary of defense on the Department of Defense.* Washington: Government Printing Office.

U.S. Bureau of the Budget. 1962. Study on Defense programming system. August 28, 1962.

U.S. Congress. House. Committee on Appropriations. *Department of Defense Appropriations for Fiscal Year 1965. Hearings before the Subcommittee on Defense Appropriations,* 88th Cong., 2nd. sess., 1964.

U.S. Congress. House. Committee on Appropriations. *Department of Defense Appropriations for Fiscal Year 1966. Hearings before the Subcommittee on Defense Appropriations*, 89th Cong., 1st sess., 1965.

U.S. Congress. Joint Economic Committee. *Planning-Programming-Budgeting: Progress and Potentials. Hearings before the Subcommittee on Economy in Government*, 90th Cong., 1st sess., 1967.

U.S. Congress. Senate. Committee on Appropriations. *Department of Defense Appropriations for Fiscal Year 1967*, 89th Cong., 2nd sess., 1966.

U.S. Congress. Senate. Committee on Government Operations. *Organizing for National Security. Hearings before the Subcommittee on National Policy Machinery*, 87th Cong., 1st sess., 1961.

U.S. Department of Defense. *Significant Documents on PPBS: Historical Milestones 1961 to 1969.* n.d.

U.S. Department of Defense. Office of the Secretary of Defense. 1965. Record of meeting on DOD FY 1967 budget (Nov. 9, 1965). November 10, 1965.

U.S. Department of Defense. 1966. Assistant Secretary of Defense, Comptroller. Memorandum on FY 1967 Supplemental and FY 1968 Budget Estimates. August 30, 1966.

U.S. Department of Defense. Directorate for Statistical Services. 1969. *Selected Manpower Statistics*, April 15, 1969.

Weidenbaum, Murray L. 1970. Institutional obstacles to reallocating government expenditures. In *Public expenditures and policy analysis*, ed. Robert H. Haveman and Julius Margolis. Chicago: Markham.

White, Paul N. 1974. Resources as determinants of organizational behavior. *Administrative Sciences Quarterly* 19:366–79.

Wildavsky, Aaron. 1968. Budgeting as a political process. In *International encyclopedia of the social sciences*, ed. David L. Sills. New York: Macmillan and The Free Press.

———. **1970.** Rescuing policy analysis from PPBS. In *Public expenditures and policy analysis*, ed. Robert H. Haveman and Julius Margolis. Chicago: Markham.

Wilensky, Harold L. 1967. *Organizational intelligence.* New York: Basic Books.

York, Herbert. 1970. *Race to oblivion.* New York: Simon and Schuster.

Index

ABM. *See* Anti-ballistic missiles

Air Force: commands of, 108; cuts in dominant services of, 66–68; dominance of, during Eisenhower administration, 30–33, 38–40, 109–10 (*see also* Eisenhower administration, New Look of); Eisenhower's defensive strategy for, 132 n.12; intraservice distinctions in, 18–20; postwar organizational strategies of, 100–101; promotions process in, 102–5, 107–8, 113–14, 138 n.16–17; response of, to 1960s defense budgets, 36–37, 42–43

Air Force Academy, 127 n.11

Allocational discretion, 13

Annapolis, 20, 127 n.9 (chap. 2)

Anti-ballistic missiles, 54–55, 128 n.6

Armed services: congressional funding for, 39–44 (*tables*); defense policy made in, 137 n.6; expertise of, 28, 49–50, 52–53 (*see also* Functional authority); independence of, 11, 16–17, 92–93; interservice rivalries among, 24–30, 34, 35–37, 42–44, 89–94; intraservice distinctions in, 18–20, 127 n.5–8; organizational boundaries between, 14–17; parochial responses of, to organizational environment, 99–102; presidential budget requests for, *table* 31; promotions process in, 102–8, 113–14, 115–17, 138 n. 16–17; reduction in budget requests by, rank-ordered, *table* 33; relative importance of, 5; and the separation of powers, 37–38; shares of budget changes in, rank-ordered, *table* 32;

shares of budget reductions in, *table* 64; shares of discretionary resources alloted to, *table* 35; treatment of, during Vietnam War, 56. *See also* Air Force; Army; Civil-military bargaining; Joint Chiefs of Staff; Navy

Army: funding for, under Eisenhower, 36–37, 41–42; intraservice distinctions in, 18–20; noncompliance of, with counterinsurgency tactics, 46; preferential treatment of, during Vietnam War, 33–34; "performance budget" of, 5; relative homogeneity of, 19, 138 n.11. *See also* Armed Services

"Assured destruction" doctrine, 83

Authority. *See* Formal authority; Functional authority

Aviators: organizational strategies of, 137 n.9; promotion opportunities of, *tables* 105–9, 110–11; service loyalties of, 18

BOB. *See* Bureau of the Budget

B-52 bomber wing: concessions regarding, 48; funds for, impounded, 42

B-70. *See* Follow-on manned bomber

Budgeting: for defense (*see* Defense budget); formats for, 10–11; importance of analysis of, 3, 10–13; organizational primacy of, 3–4

Bureaucracy. *See* Organization theory

Bureau of the Budget, 77, 126 n.5

Chu, David, 102

Civil-military bargaining: armed services advantages in (*see* Armed services, expertise of;

Civil-military bargaining (*cont.*)
Functional authority); civilian concessions in, 47–51, 119–20; direct confrontation in, 54–57 (*see also* McNamara, bargaining by, with military leaders); necessity for, 81, 108–19; "personnel approach" to, 95–98; and PPBS, 85–94, 135 n.11; presidential advantages in, 51–52, 81, 84–85, 95, 108–15, 119–23 passim; role of allocation rivalries in, 89–91

Combat, 19, 127 n.5–8

Compliance. *See* Civil-military bargaining

Congress: Air Force support by, during 1960s, 43–44; appropriations of, as percentage of president's budget request, *table* 40; and the Eisenhower administration, 38–40, 129 n.11; general role of, in defense bargaining, 37–38, 44; impact of, on Joint Chiefs of Staff dissension, 42; personnel and procurement funding by, *table* 39; relative funding of armed services by, *table* 41

Crecine, John P., 62, 75, 125 n.2

Cuban missile crisis: limits on presidential power in, 1; and McNamara, 135 n.5; strategic options in, 130 n.8

"Damage limitation" doctrine, 83

Davis, Vincent: on Eisenhower's military expertise, 23; on intraservice distinctions, 18–19; on McNamara's value to Kennedy, 87; on Naval aviators, 18–19, 100–101, 137 n.9

Defense budget: allocational discretion in, 13, 131 n.2; amendments and supplementals to, 7, 9, 127 n.9 (chap. 1), 130 n.5; ceilings on, 74–77, 88, 90, 93, 122, 131 n.2,6, 133 n.18; as civilian control tool over the military, 6, 24–25, 30–33, 111–14; as civil-military nexus, 2; constraints on, during Vietnam War, 56–57; of Eisenhower, criticized, 59–61, 74, 131 n.3; for fiscal year 1968, 54–55; levels of, and Joint Chiefs of Staff dissension, 24–26; "line item" format of, 7–9; under McNamara (*see* Five Year Defense Plan; Planning-Programming-Budgeting System); OSD share of, *table* 80; and promotion opportunities, 111–14; as quantitative statement of military policy, 4–6, 10–13 passim, 30–32; role of compromise in, 9

Defense Intelligence Agency, 49, 53–54

Delegation: by the Joint Chiefs of Staff, 26–27; by the president, 45, 118–19

Department of Defense. *See* Defense budget; Office of the Secretary of Defense; and *names of specific secretaries for defense*

Dynasoar, 42–43

Eberstadt, Ferdinand, 6

Eisenhower administration: Air Force dominance during, 30–33, 38–40, 109–10 (*see also* New Look); appointments to Joint Chiefs of Staff by, 95–97, 136 n.1; bargaining by, with military leaders, 85–87, 90, 135 n.7; budgetary criticisms of, 58–61, 74; concessions of, to Joint Chiefs of Staff, 47–48, 53; and Congress, 38–40, 129 n.11; defense budget cutting by, empirically studied, 62–68; fiscal years of, 7; interservice rivalry during, 25; "New Look" of, 38–40, 97, 109–10, 132 n.11–12, 137 n.6; rejections of Joint Chiefs of Staff positions by, 54; strategic doctrines of, 81–82, 109–10; use of budget by, 24–25, 62–70

Enthoven, Alain: on Eisenhower's budgeting, 59, 61, 131 n.3; on Five Year Defense Program, 71, 133 n.17

Firepower strategy, 38–39
Five Year Defense Program: as mission-oriented budget structure, 60; shortcomings of, 72–74, 83–84, 121–22, 133 n.15; and subordinate compliance monitoring, 71–72, 74. *See also* Planning-Programming-Budgeting System
Flexible response doctrine, 82–83, 110, 137 n.6
Follow-on manned bomber: disputes about, 54–55, 83, 93, 135 n.9; rejection, 42, 54
Formal authority, 84–85, 95, 118 (*see also* Civil-military bargaining, presidential advantages in)
Frank, Forest, 55
Functional authority 84–89, 135 n.6 (*see also* Civil-military bargaining, armed services advantage in)
FYDP. *See* Five Year Defense Program

Halperin, Morton, 99, 137 n.8
Hammond, Paul Y.: on civilian-military bargaining, 51; on Defense comptrollership, 69; on Eisenhower's budget mechanisms, 134 n.20; on McNamara's systems analysis, 87
Health, Education, and Welfare (HEW), 13
Hitch, Charles: on armed services, rivalries, 92; on Eisenhower's defense budgeting, 59–61; on the Five Year Defense Program, 73; on PPBS, 61, 75; on weapons systems budgeting, 68
Hoover Commission: on the budget's importance, 6; on defense comptrollership, 69
Huntington, Samuel P., 30, 34, 44

Input budgeting, 10–11

JCS. *See* Joint Chiefs of Staff
Johnson administration: bargaining by, with military leaders (*see* McNamara, Robert, bargaining by); and Eisenhower administration, compared, 77; Five Year Defense Program during, 74, 133 n.16; interservice rivalry during, 25, 43; and the Vietnam War, 46–47
Joint Chiefs of Staff: administrative overtures to, 25, 47–51; agenda of, 128 n.2, 130 n.9; appointment of, by the president, 95–99; arena for military negotiations, 15, 25; claims to expertise by, 28, 49–50, 52–53 (*see also* Functional authority); consensus among, 25–28, 36, 44, 53, 93–94; decision-making by, 25–30; dissension among, 25–26, 28–30, 34, 35–37, 42, 53, 55 (*see also* Armed services, interservice rivalries among); political importance of, 25, 44, 48–50, 53. *See also* Armed services; Civil-military bargaining
Jones, William, 29

Kaufman, Herbert, 127 n.1
Kaufmann, William: on flexible response, 82; on McNamara's control devices, 71–72
Kennedy administration: bargaining by, with military leaders (*see* McNamara, Robert, bargaining by); congressional funding during, 43; and the Cuban missile crisis, 1; defense budget increases during, 42; and the Eisenhower administration, compared, 77; interservice rivalry during, 25, 42–43; and the Joint Chiefs of Staff, 96–97; presidential campaign of, 74; relative status of armed services during, *tables* 31–33, 110; strategic doctrine of, 82–83, 110–11
Kennedy, Robert, 1, 130 n.8

Kissinger, Henry: on aggregate defense appropriations, 5; on new ideas in Washington, 137 n.6; on presidential power, 125 n.1
Komer, Robert, 46
Kuzmack, Arnold, 134 n.18

Laird, Melvin, 112, 122
Legere, Lawrence: on Eisenhower's military expertise, 23; on McNamara's value to Kennedy, 87
LeMay, Curtis: bargaining by, in Joint Chiefs of Staff, 130 n.10; bargaining by, for larger budgets, 136 n.13; conflicts of, with Gen. Taylor, 55, 128 n.6
Lemnitzer, Lyman, 96–97
Longley, Charles, 128 n.3

McNamara, Robert: administrative problems of, summarized, 122; on Air Force funding, 42; bargaining by, with military leaders, 85–94, 120, 135 n.11; on budgetary connotations, 5; and ceilings for defense spending, 74–77, 88, 90, 93, 122; concessions by, to Joint Chiefs of Staff, 47–49, 53–54; confrontations of, with Joint Chiefs of Staff, 54–57; legacy of, 123; management systems "revolution" under, 2, 4, 6–7, 60, 131 n.3 (see also Planning-Programming-Budgeting System); and military uniforms, 16; use of systems analysis by, 87–88, 135 n.9. See also Five Year Defense Plan; Office of the Secretary of Defense
McNeil, Wilfred, 70
Mahon, George, 129 n.4, 132 n.12
Manned bomber, 42–43. See also Follow-on manned bomber
Manpower strategy, 38–39
March, James G., 14
Massive retaliation doctrine, 81–82, 109–10

Military, 15. See also Armed services; Defense budget; Joint Chiefs of Staff
Military Airlift Command, 108
Military construction, 9
Military officers: education of, tables 21–22, 127 n.9 (chap. 2); familiarity of, with budget data, 4; line vs. staff distinctions in, 137 n.11; promotion process of, 102–8,113–14, 115–17, 138 n.16–17; "secondary zone" of, 138 n.16,20
Military personnel: congressional funding for, 39–40; line items in, 8; presidential appointment of, 95–99
Millis, Walter, 6
Mosher, Frederick: on defense budget, 13; on organizational budgets, 3

National security: cost calculations of, by McNamara, 133 n. 18; priorities for, reflected in budgets, 5–6 (see also Defense budget); and presidential delegation, 45, 118–19; use of organizational theory in, 118–23 passim
National Security Act of 1947, 6; 1947 amendments to, 6; 1958 amendments to, 16–17, 37
Navy: annual Register of, 127 n.9 (chap. 2); aviators in, 105–7, 110–11, 113–14, 116, 137 n. 9; cuts in dominant branch in, 67–68, 132 n.10; intraservice distinctions in, 18–20; postwar organizational strategies of, 100–101; promotions process in, 102–7, 113–14, 115–17, 138 n.16; resistance to budgetary change by, 5. See also Armed Services
Neustadt, Richard E., 1, 37, 52, 118, 137 n.7
New Look: air strategies of, 132 n.12; congressional fostering of, 38–40; dominant features of,

38; fiscal constraints in, 132 n. 11; vs. flexible response, 137 n.6; and the Joint Chiefs of Staff, 97; and military promotions, 109–10

New Obligational Authority, 131 n.6

Niskanen, William, 11

Nixon, Richard M., 5

NOA. *See* New Obligational Authority

Noncompliance. *See* Civil-military bargaining

Nuclear weaponry. *See* Strategic doctrines

Office of the Secretary of Defense, 6–7, 79–80, 91, 122, 134 n.1–2

Operations and maintenance: line items in, 8; as locus of budget cuts, 66, 132 n.8

Organization theory: budgetary perspectives in, 3, 10–13; concept of boundaries in, 14 (*see also* Armed Services, interservice rivalries in); of the executive task, 45; importance of, to national security leadership, 118–23; of intraorganizational leadership, 99–100; official vs. operative goals in, 137 n.10; of personnel parochialism, 98; of subordinate noncompliance, 45–47

OSD. *See* Office of Secretary of Defense

Output budgeting, 11

Pacific Air Forces (PACOM), 17, 108

Packard, David, 4

Peabody, Robert L., 84

Perrow, Charles: on organizational goals, 137 n.10; on sources of organizational leadership, 100–101

Personnel, budget analyses of, 12 (*see also* Military personnel)

Planning-Programming-Budgeting System: and bargaining with the military, 85–94 passim, 120, 135 n.11; component mechanisms of, 131 n.4; functional similarity of, to Eisenhower budgeting, 70–71, 77–78, 121, 139 n.23; inadequacies of, summarized, 121–22; as output budgeting, 11; as tool for budgetary reform, 6, 24–25, 58–61. *See also* Five Year Defense Program; McNamara, Robert

Presidency: and armed service boundaries, 14–15; formal authority of, 84–85, 95, 118; limits on power of, 1, 45–47, 50, 81, 118–19, 125 n.1; management of military staff by, 95–99, 99–102 passim, 108–15. *See also* Civil-military bargaining; *and names of specific presidential administrations*

Procurement: and budget cuts, 66–67, 132 n.8; congressional funding for, during Eisenhower administration, 39–40; line items in, 8

Quester, George, 133 n.12

Radford, Arthur, 96–97, 136 n.3

Research, Development, Test and Evaluation: line items in, 8–9; McNamara's use of, 57; relative immunity of, to budget cuts, 132 n.8

Ridgway, Matthew, 97, 135 n.7–8

Riordan, Stephen, 5

Rivers, Mendel, 43

Rowen, Henry, 83

Secretary of Defense. *See* Office of the Secretary of Defense; *and names of specific secretaries*

Segel, David R., 20

Separation of powers, 37–38

Service academies: and flag-grade rank, *tables* 21–22; and military socialization, 19–20

Simon, Herbert A., 14

Skybolt: and Kennedy administration, 43, 130 n.5; Gen. Taylor's opposition to, 128 n.6
Smith, K. Wayne: on Eisenhower's budgeting, 61, 131 n.3; on Five Year Defense Program, 71, 133 n.17
Smith, Perry, 18–19, 100–101, 127 n.4
Snyder, Glenn, 82, 136 n.3–4
Sorenson, Theodore, 96
State Department, budgetary analysis in, 12
Strategic air command, 108–10, 113–14, 138 n.20
Strategic doctrines: Eisenhower's use of, 38–40, 81–82, 97, 109–10, 132 n.11–12, 137 n.6; formulation of, 134 n.3; Kennedy's use of, 82–83, 110–11; role of, in officers' promotions, 108–11; Truman's use of, 82, 134 n.3
Stromberg, John, 126 n.6, 133 n.14
Submarines, 12, 54–55
Systems analysis, 87–88, 92

Tactical Air Command, 108, 112, 130 n.8
Taft, Robert, 136 n.1
Taylor, Maxwell: conflicts of, with Gen. LeMay, 55, 128 n.6; as critic of Eisenhower, 69, 96–97, 136 n.2; on interservice rivalry, 136 n.15; on Joint Chiefs of Staff responsibilities, 38; on rejections of Joint Chiefs of Staff recommendations, 54; role of, under Kennedy administration, 96–97
Technology and interservice rivalries, 136 n.15

Thompson, Victor, 84
Truman administration: budget ceiling during, 131 n.2; strategic doctrine of, 82

Uniforms: for differentiation, 18; as symbols, 16
U.S. Air Forces Europe (EUCOM), 17, 108
U.S. Blue Ribbon Defense Panel, 17, 75, 127 n.2, 128 n.4

Vietnam War: beginning of, 7; budgetary constraints during, 55–57; budgetary disputes over, 54–55; failure of counterinsurgency tactics in, 46; military buildup for, and Joint Chiefs of Staff rivalries, 25–26; relative status of armed services during, *tables* 31–33, 35; withdrawal from, 112

Weapons systems. See Procurement; *and names of specific military technologies*
Weidenbaum, Murray, 13
West Point, 20
Wheeler, Earle: as Chairman of the Joint Chiefs of Staff, 97; and interservice cooperation, 55; on separation of powers, 37–38
White, John, 102
Wildavsky, Aaron, 127 n.9 (chap. 1)
Wilson, Charles: and budget ceilings, 131 n.6, 133 n.18; leadership style of, 22–23; and Adm. Radford, 136 n.3